Satires of Circumstance, Lyrics and Reveries, with Miscellaneous Pieces

Thomas Hardy

Contents

SATIRES OF CIRCUMSTANCE, LYRICS AND REVERIES, WITH MISCELLANEOUS PIECES

BY

Thomas Hardy

IN FRONT OF THE LANDSCAPE

Plunging and labouring on in a tide of visions,
   Dolorous and dear,
Forward I pushed my way as amid waste waters
   Stretching around,
Through whose eddies there glimmered the customed landscape
   Yonder and near,

Blotted to feeble mist. And the coomb and the upland
   Foliage-crowned,
Ancient chalk-pit, milestone, rills in the grass-flat
   Stroked by the light,
Seemed but a ghost-like gauze, and no substantial
   Meadow or mound.

What were the infinite spectacles bulking foremost
   Under my sight,
Hindering me to discern my paced advancement
   Lengthening to miles;
What were the re-creations killing the daytime
   As by the night?

O they were speechful faces, gazing insistent,
   Some as with smiles,

Some as with slow-born tears that brinily trundled
  Over the wrecked
Cheeks that were fair in their flush-time, ash now with anguish,
  Harrowed by wiles.

Yes, I could see them, feel them, hear them, address them -
  Halo-bedecked -
And, alas, onwards, shaken by fierce unreason,
  Rigid in hate,
Smitten by years-long wryness born of misprision,
  Dreaded, suspect.

Then there would breast me shining sights, sweet seasons
  Further in date;
Instruments of strings with the tenderest passion
  Vibrant, beside
Lamps long extinguished, robes, cheeks, eyes with the earth's crust
  Now corporate.

Also there rose a headland of hoary aspect
  Gnawed by the tide,
Frilled by the nimb of the morning as two friends stood there
  Guilelessly glad -
Wherefore they knew not--touched by the fringe of an ecstasy
  Scantly descried.

Later images too did the day unfurl me,
  Shadowed and sad,
Clay cadavers of those who had shared in the dramas,
  Laid now at ease,
Passions all spent, chiefest the one of the broad brow
  Sepulture-clad.

So did beset me scenes miscalled of the bygone,
  Over the leaze,
Past the clump, and down to where lay the beheld ones;
  --Yea, as the rhyme
Sung by the sea-swell, so in their pleading dumbness
  Captured me these.

For, their lost revisiting manifestations
  In their own time
Much had I slighted, caring not for their purport,
  Seeing behind
Things more coveted, reckoned the better worth calling
  Sweet, sad, sublime.

Thus do they now show hourly before the intenser
  Stare of the mind
As they were ghosts avenging their slights by my bypast
  Body-borne eyes,
Show, too, with fuller translation than rested upon them
  As living kind.

Hence wag the tongues of the passing people, saying
  In their surmise,
"Ah--whose is this dull form that perambulates, seeing nought
  Round him that looms
Whithersoever his footsteps turn in his farings,
  Save a few tombs?"

CHANNEL FIRING

That night your great guns, unawares,
Shook all our coffins as we lay,
And broke the chancel window-squares,
We thought it was the Judgment-day

And sat upright. While drearisome
Arose the howl of wakened hounds:
The mouse let fall the altar-crumb,
The worms drew back into the mounds,

The glebe cow drooled. Till God called, "No;
It's gunnery practice out at sea
Just as before you went below;
The world is as it used to be:

"All nations striving strong to make
Red war yet redder. Mad as hatters
They do no more for Christes sake
Than you who are helpless in such matters.

"That this is not the judgment-hour
For some of them's a blessed thing,
For if it were they'd have to scour
Hell's floor for so much threatening . . .

"Ha, ha. It will be warmer when
I blow the trumpet (if indeed
I ever do; for you are men,

And rest eternal sorely need).”

So down we lay again. “I wonder,
Will the world ever saner be,”
Said one, “than when He sent us under
In our indifferent century!”

And many a skeleton shook his head.
“Instead of preaching forty year,”
My neighbour Parson Thirdly said,
“I wish I had stuck to pipes and beer.”

Again the guns disturbed the hour,
Roaring their readiness to avenge,
As far inland as Stourton Tower,
And Camelot, and starlit Stonehenge.

April 1914.

THE CONVERGENCE OF THE TWAIN

(Lines on the loss of the "Titanic")

I

  In a solitude of the sea
   Deep from human vanity,
And the Pride of Life that planned her, stilly couches she.

II

  Steel chambers, late the pyres
   Of her salamandrine fires,
Cold currents thrid, and turn to rhythmic tidal lyres.

III

  Over the mirrors meant
   To glass the opulent
The sea-worm crawls--grotesque, slimed, dumb, indifferent.

IV

  Jewels in joy designed
   To ravish the sensuous mind
Lie lightless, all their sparkles bleared and black and blind.

V

   Dim moon-eyed fishes near
    Gaze at the gilded gear
And query: "What does this vaingloriousness down here?" . . .

VI

   Well: while was fashioning
    This creature of cleaving wing,
The Immanent Will that stirs and urges everything

VII

   Prepared a sinister mate
    For her--so gaily great -
A Shape of Ice, for the time far and dissociate.

VIII

   And as the smart ship grew
    In stature, grace, and hue,
In shadowy silent distance grew the Iceberg too.

IX

   Alien they seemed to be:
    No mortal eye could see
The intimate welding of their later history,

X

   Or sign that they were bent

By paths coincident
On being anon twin halves of one august event,

XI

Till the Spinner of the Years
   Said "Now!" And each one hears,
And consummation comes, and jars two hemispheres.

THE GHOST OF THE PAST

We two kept house, the Past and I,
   The Past and I;
I tended while it hovered nigh,
   Leaving me never alone.
It was a spectral housekeeping
   Where fell no jarring tone,
As strange, as still a housekeeping
   As ever has been known.

As daily I went up the stair
   And down the stair,
I did not mind the Bygone there -
   The Present once to me;
Its moving meek companionship
   I wished might ever be,
There was in that companionship
   Something of ecstasy.

It dwelt with me just as it was,
   Just as it was
When first its prospects gave me pause
   In wayward wanderings,
Before the years had torn old troths
   As they tear all sweet things,
Before gaunt griefs had torn old troths
   And dulled old rapturings.

And then its form began to fade,
   Began to fade,
Its gentle echoes faintlier played
   At eves upon my ear
Than when the autumn's look embrowned
   The lonely chambers here,
The autumn's settling shades embrowned
   Nooks that it haunted near.

And so with time my vision less,
   Yea, less and less
Makes of that Past my housemistress,
   It dwindles in my eye;
It looms a far-off skeleton
   And not a comrade nigh,
A fitful far-off skeleton
   Dimming as days draw by.

AFTER THE VISIT
(To F. E. D.)

Come again to the place
Where your presence was as a leaf that skims
Down a drouthy way whose ascent bedims
  The bloom on the farer's face.

Come again, with the feet
That were light on the green as a thistledown ball,
And those mute ministrations to one and to all
  Beyond a man's saying sweet.

Until then the faint scent
Of the bordering flowers swam unheeded away,
And I marked not the charm in the changes of day
  As the cloud-colours came and went.

Through the dark corridors
Your walk was so soundless I did not know
Your form from a phantom's of long ago
  Said to pass on the ancient floors,

Till you drew from the shade,
And I saw the large luminous living eyes
Regard me in fixed inquiring-wise
  As those of a soul that weighed,

Scarce consciously,
The eternal question of what Life was,

And why we were there, and by whose strange laws
  That which mattered most could not be.

TO MEET, OR OTHERWISE

Whether to sally and see thee, girl of my dreams,
  Or whether to stay
And see thee not! How vast the difference seems
  Of Yea from Nay
Just now. Yet this same sun will slant its beams
  At no far day
On our two mounds, and then what will the difference weigh!

Yet I will see thee, maiden dear, and make
  The most I can
Of what remains to us amid this brake Cimmerian
Through which we grope, and from whose thorns we ache,
  While still we scan
Round our frail faltering progress for some path or plan.

By briefest meeting something sure is won;
  It will have been:
Nor God nor Daemon can undo the done,
  Unsight the seen,
Make muted music be as unbegun,
  Though things terrene
Groan in their bondage till oblivion supervene.

So, to the one long-sweeping symphony
    From times remote
Till now, of human tenderness, shall we
    Supply one note,
Small and untraced, yet that will ever be
    Somewhere afloat
Amid the spheres, as part of sick Life's antidote.

THE DIFFERENCE

I

Sinking down by the gate I discern the thin moon,
And a blackbird tries over old airs in the pine,
But the moon is a sorry one, sad the bird's tune,
For this spot is unknown to that Heartmate of mine.

II

Did my Heartmate but haunt here at times such as now,
The song would be joyous and cheerful the moon;
But she will see never this gate, path, or bough,
Nor I find a joy in the scene or the tune.

THE SUN ON THE BOOKCASE
(Student's Love-song)

Once more the cauldron of the sun
Smears the bookcase with winy red,
And here my page is, and there my bed,
And the apple-tree shadows travel along.
Soon their intangible track will be run,
   And dusk grow strong
   And they be fled.

Yes: now the boiling ball is gone,
And I have wasted another day . . .
But wasted--WASTED, do I say?
Is it a waste to have imaged one
Beyond the hills there, who, anon,
   My great deeds done
   Will be mine alway?

"WHEN I SET OUT FOR LYONNESSE"

When I set out for Lyonnesse,
  A hundred miles away,
  The rime was on the spray,
And starlight lit my lonesomeness
When I set out for Lyonnesse
  A hundred miles away.

What would bechance at Lyonnesse
  While I should sojourn there
  No prophet durst declare,
Nor did the wisest wizard guess
What would bechance at Lyonnesse
  While I should sojourn there.

When I came back from Lyonnesse
  With magic in my eyes,
  None managed to surmise
What meant my godlike gloriousness,
When I came back from Lyonnesse
  With magic in my eyes.

A THUNDERSTORM IN TOWN
(A Reminiscence)

She wore a new "terra-cotta" dress,
And we stayed, because of the pelting storm,
Within the hansom's dry recess,
Though the horse had stopped; yea, motionless
  We sat on, snug and warm.

Then the downpour ceased, to my sharp sad pain,
And the glass that had screened our forms before
Flew up, and out she sprang to her door:
I should have kissed her if the rain
  Had lasted a minute more.

THE TORN LETTER

I

I tore your letter into strips
  No bigger than the airy feathers
  That ducks preen out in changing weathers
Upon the shifting ripple-tips.

II

In darkness on my bed alone
  I seemed to see you in a vision,
  And hear you say: "Why this derision
Of one drawn to you, though unknown?"

III

Yes, eve's quick mood had run its course,
  The night had cooled my hasty madness;
  I suffered a regretful sadness
Which deepened into real remorse.

IV

I thought what pensive patient days
  A soul must know of grain so tender,
  How much of good must grace the sender
Of such sweet words in such bright phrase.

V

Uprising then, as things unpriced
  I sought each fragment, patched and mended;
  The midnight whitened ere I had ended
And gathered words I had sacrificed.

VI

But some, alas, of those I threw
  Were past my search, destroyed for ever:
  They were your name and place; and never

Did I regain those clues to you.

VII

I learnt I had missed, by rash unheed,
  My track; that, so the Will decided,
  In life, death, we should be divided,
And at the sense I ached indeed.

VIII

That ache for you, born long ago,
  Throbs on; I never could outgrow it.
  What a revenge, did you but know it!
But that, thank God, you do not know.

BEYOND THE LAST LAMP
(Near Tooting Common)

I

While rain, with eve in partnership,
Descended darkly, drip, drip, drip,
Beyond the last lone lamp I passed
  Walking slowly, whispering sadly,
  Two linked loiterers, wan, downcast:
Some heavy thought constrained each face,
And blinded them to time and place.

II

The pair seemed lovers, yet absorbed
In mental scenes no longer orbed
By love's young rays. Each countenance
   As it slowly, as it sadly
   Caught the lamplight's yellow glance
Held in suspense a misery
At things which had been or might be.

III

When I retrod that watery way
Some hours beyond the droop of day,
Still I found pacing there the twain
   Just as slowly, just as sadly,
   Heedless of the night and rain.
One could but wonder who they were
And what wild woe detained them there.

IV

Though thirty years of blur and blot
Have slid since I beheld that spot,
And saw in curious converse there
   Moving slowly, moving sadly
   That mysterious tragic pair,
Its olden look may linger on -
All but the couple; they have gone.

V

Whither? Who knows, indeed . . . And yet

To me, when nights are weird and wet,
Without those comrades there at tryst
  Creeping slowly, creeping sadly,
  That lone lane does not exist.
There they seem brooding on their pain,
And will, while such a lane remain.

THE FACE AT THE CASEMENT

  If ever joy leave
An abiding sting of sorrow,
So befell it on the morrow
  Of that May eve . . .

  The travelled sun dropped
To the north-west, low and lower,
The pony's trot grew slower,
  And then we stopped.

  "This cosy house just by
I must call at for a minute,
A sick man lies within it
  Who soon will die.

  "He wished to marry me,
So I am bound, when I drive near him,
To inquire, if but to cheer him,
  How he may be."

A message was sent in,
And wordlessly we waited,
Till some one came and stated
  The bulletin.

And that the sufferer said,
For her call no words could thank her;
As his angel he must rank her
  Till life's spark fled.

Slowly we drove away,
When I turned my head, although not
Called; why so I turned I know not
  Even to this day.

And lo, there in my view
Pressed against an upper lattice
Was a white face, gazing at us
  As we withdrew.

And well did I divine
It to be the man's there dying,
Who but lately had been sighing
  For her pledged mine.

Then I deigned a deed of hell;
It was done before I knew it;
What devil made me do it
  I cannot tell!

Yes, while he gazed above,
I put my arm about her
That he might see, nor doubt her

My plighted Love.

The pale face vanished quick,
As if blasted, from the casement,
And my shame and self-abasement
  Began their prick.

And they prick on, ceaselessly,
For that stab in Love's fierce fashion
Which, unfired by lover's passion,
  Was foreign to me.

She smiled at my caress,
But why came the soft embowment
Of her shoulder at that moment
  She did not guess.

Long long years has he lain
In thy garth, O sad Saint Cleather:
What tears there, bared to weather,
  Will cleanse that stain!

Love is long-suffering, brave,
Sweet, prompt, precious as a jewel;
But O, too, Love is cruel,
  Cruel as the grave.

LOST LOVE

I play my sweet old airs -
  The airs he knew
  When our love was true -
  But he does not balk
  His determined walk,
And passes up the stairs.

I sing my songs once more,
  And presently hear
  His footstep near
  As if it would stay;
  But he goes his way,
And shuts a distant door.

So I wait for another morn
  And another night
  In this soul-sick blight;
  And I wonder much
  As I sit, why such
A woman as I was born!

"MY SPIRIT WILL NOT HAUNT THE MOUND"

My spirit will not haunt the mound
  Above my breast,
But travel, memory-possessed,
To where my tremulous being found
  Life largest, best.

My phantom-footed shape will go
  When nightfall grays
Hither and thither along the ways
I and another used to know
  In backward days.

And there you'll find me, if a jot
  You still should care
For me, and for my curious air;
If otherwise, then I shall not,
  For you, be there.

WESSEX HEIGHTS (1896)

There are some heights in Wessex, shaped as if by a kindly hand
For thinking, dreaming, dying on, and at crises when I stand,
Say, on Ingpen Beacon eastward, or on Wylls-Neck westwardly,
I seem where I was before my birth, and after death may be.

In the lowlands I have no comrade, not even the lone man's friend -
Her who suffereth long and is kind; accepts what he is too weak to
mend:
Down there they are dubious and askance; there nobody thinks as I,
But mind-chains do not clank where one's next neighbour is the sky.

In the towns I am tracked by phantoms having weird detective ways -
Shadows of beings who fellowed with myself of earlier days:
They hang about at places, and they say harsh heavy things -
Men with a frigid sneer, and women with tart disparagings.

Down there I seem to be false to myself, my simple self that was,
And is not now, and I see him watching, wondering what crass cause
Can have merged him into such a strange continuator as this,
Who yet has something in common with himself, my chrysalis.

I cannot go to the great grey Plain; there's a figure against the
moon,
Nobody sees it but I, and it makes my breast beat out of tune;
I cannot go to the tall-spired town, being barred by the forms now
passed
For everybody but me, in whose long vision they stand there fast.

There's a ghost at Yell'ham Bottom chiding loud at the fall of the
night,
There's a ghost in Froom-side Vale, thin lipped and vague, in a
shroud of white,
There is one in the railway-train whenever I do not want it near,
I see its profile against the pane, saying what I would not hear.

As for one rare fair woman, I am now but a thought of hers,
I enter her mind and another thought succeeds me that she prefers;
Yet my love for her in its fulness she herself even did not know;

Well, time cures hearts of tenderness, and now I can let her go.

So I am found on Ingpen Beacon, or on Wylls-Neck to the west,
Or else on homely Bulbarrow, or little Pilsdon Crest,
Where men have never cared to haunt, nor women have walked with me,
And ghosts then keep their distance; and I know some liberty.

IN DEATH DIVIDED

I

I shall rot here, with those whom in their day
   You never knew,
And alien ones who, ere they chilled to clay,
   Met not my view,
Will in your distant grave-place ever neighbour you.

II

No shade of pinnacle or tree or tower,
   While earth endures,
Will fall on my mound and within the hour
   Steal on to yours;
One robin never haunt our two green covertures.

III

Some organ may resound on Sunday noons
   By where you lie,
Some other thrill the panes with other tunes

Where moulder I;
No selfsame chords compose our common lullaby.

IV

The simply-cut memorial at my head
   Perhaps may take
A Gothic form, and that above your bed
   Be Greek in make;
No linking symbol show thereon for our tale's sake.

V

And in the monotonous moils of strained, hard-run
   Humanity,
The eternal tie which binds us twain in one
   No eye will see
Stretching across the miles that sever you from me.

THE PLACE ON THE MAP

I

I look upon the map that hangs by me -
Its shires and towns and rivers lined in varnished artistry -
   And I mark a jutting height
Coloured purple, with a margin of blue sea.

II

--'Twas a day of latter summer, hot and dry;
Ay, even the waves seemed drying as we walked on, she and I,
    By this spot where, calmly quite,
She informed me what would happen by and by.

III

    This hanging map depicts the coast and place,
And resuscitates therewith our unexpected troublous case
    All distinctly to my sight,
And her tension, and the aspect of her face.

IV

    Weeks and weeks we had loved beneath that blazing blue,
Which had lost the art of raining, as her eyes to-day had too,
    While she told what, as by sleight,
Shot our firmament with rays of ruddy hue.

V

    For the wonder and the wormwood of the whole
Was that what in realms of reason would have joyed our double soul
    Wore a torrid tragic light
Under order-keeping's rigorous control.

VI

    So, the map revives her words, the spot, the time,
And the thing we found we had to face before the next year's prime;
    The charted coast stares bright,

And its episode comes back in pantomime.

WHERE THE PICNIC WAS

Where we made the fire,
In the summer time,
Of branch and briar
On the hill to the sea
I slowly climb
Through winter mire,
And scan and trace
The forsaken place
Quite readily.

Now a cold wind blows,
And the grass is gray,
But the spot still shows
As a burnt circle--aye,
And stick-ends, charred,
Still strew the sward
Whereon I stand,
Last relic of the band
Who came that day!

Yes, I am here
Just as last year,
And the sea breathes brine
From its strange straight line
Up hither, the same
As when we four came.

- But two have wandered far
From this grassy rise
Into urban roar
Where no picnics are,
And one--has shut her eyes
For evermore.

THE SCHRECKHORN
(With thoughts of Leslie Stephen)
(June 1897)

Aloof, as if a thing of mood and whim;
Now that its spare and desolate figure gleams
Upon my nearing vision, less it seems
A looming Alp-height than a guise of him
Who scaled its horn with ventured life and limb,
Drawn on by vague imaginings, maybe,
Of semblance to his personality
In its quaint glooms, keen lights, and rugged trim.

At his last change, when Life's dull coils unwind,
Will he, in old love, hitherward escape,
And the eternal essence of his mind
Enter this silent adamantine shape,
And his low voicing haunt its slipping snows
When dawn that calls the climber dyes them rose?

A SINGER ASLEEP
(Algernon Charles Swinburne, 1837-1909)

I

In this fair niche above the unslumbering sea,
That sentrys up and down all night, all day,
From cove to promontory, from ness to bay,
   The Fates have fitly bidden that he should be Pillowed eternally.

II

- It was as though a garland of red roses
Had fallen about the hood of some smug nun
When irresponsibly dropped as from the sun,
In fulth of numbers freaked with musical closes,
Upon Victoria's formal middle time
   His leaves of rhythm and rhyme.

III

O that far morning of a summer day
When, down a terraced street whose pavements lay
Glassing the sunshine into my bent eyes,
I walked and read with a quick glad surprise
   New words, in classic guise, -

IV

The passionate pages of his earlier years,
Fraught with hot sighs, sad laughters, kisses, tears;

Fresh-fluted notes, yet from a minstrel who
Blew them not naively, but as one who knew
    Full well why thus he blew.

V

I still can hear the brabble and the roar
At those thy tunes, O still one, now passed through
That fitful fire of tongues then entered new!
Their power is spent like spindrift on this shore;
    Thine swells yet more and more.

VI

- His singing-mistress verily was no other
Than she the Lesbian, she the music-mother
Of all the tribe that feel in melodies;
Who leapt, love-anguished, from the Leucadian steep
Into the rambling world-encircling deep
    Which hides her where none sees.

VII

And one can hold in thought that nightly here
His phantom may draw down to the water's brim,
And hers come up to meet it, as a dim
Lone shine upon the heaving hydrosphere,
And mariners wonder as they traverse near,
    Unknowing of her and him.

VIII

One dreams him sighing to her spectral form:
"O teacher, where lies hid thy burning line;
Where are those songs, O poetess divine
Whose very arts are love incarnadine?"
And her smile back: "Disciple true and warm,
  Sufficient now are thine." . . .

IX

So here, beneath the waking constellations,
Where the waves peal their everlasting strains,
And their dull subterrene reverberations
Shake him when storms make mountains of their plains -
Him once their peer in sad improvisations,
And deft as wind to cleave their frothy manes -
I leave him, while the daylight gleam declines
  Upon the capes and chines.

BONCHURCH, 1910.

A PLAINT TO MAN

When you slowly emerged from the den of Time,
And gained percipience as you grew,
And fleshed you fair out of shapeless slime,

Wherefore, O Man, did there come to you
The unhappy need of creating me -
A form like your own--for praying to?

My virtue, power, utility,
Within my maker must all abide,
Since none in myself can ever be,

One thin as a shape on a lantern-slide
Shown forth in the dark upon some dim sheet,
And by none but its showman vivified.

"Such a forced device," you may say, "is meet
For easing a loaded heart at whiles:
Man needs to conceive of a mercy-seat

Somewhere above the gloomy aisles
Of this wailful world, or he could not bear
The irk no local hope beguiles."

- But since I was framed in your first despair
The doing without me has had no play
In the minds of men when shadows scare;

And now that I dwindle day by day
Beneath the deicide eyes of seers
In a light that will not let me stay,

And to-morrow the whole of me disappears,
The truth should be told, and the fact be faced
That had best been faced in earlier years:

The fact of life with dependence placed
On the human heart's resource alone,
In brotherhood bonded close and graced

With loving-kindness fully blown,
And visioned help unsought, unknown.

1909-10.

GOD'S FUNERAL

I

   I saw a slowly-stepping train -
Lined on the brows, scoop-eyed and bent and hoar -
Following in files across a twilit plain
A strange and mystic form the foremost bore.

II

   And by contagious throbs of thought
Or latent knowledge that within me lay

And had already stirred me, I was wrought
To consciousness of sorrow even as they.

III

  The fore-borne shape, to my blurred eyes,
At first seemed man-like, and anon to change
To an amorphous cloud of marvellous size,
At times endowed with wings of glorious range.

IV

  And this phantasmal variousness
Ever possessed it as they drew along:
Yet throughout all it symboled none the less
Potency vast and loving-kindness strong.

V

  Almost before I knew I bent
Towards the moving columns without a word;
They, growing in bulk and numbers as they went,
Struck out sick thoughts that could be overheard:-

VI

  "O man-projected Figure, of late
Imaged as we, thy knell who shall survive?
Whence came it we were tempted to create
One whom we can no longer keep alive?

VII

"Framing him jealous, fierce, at first,
We gave him justice as the ages rolled,
Will to bless those by circumstance accurst,
And longsuffering, and mercies manifold.

VIII

"And, tricked by our own early dream
And need of solace, we grew self-deceived,
Our making soon our maker did we deem,
And what we had imagined we believed.

IX

"Till, in Time's stayless stealthy swing,
Uncompromising rude reality
Mangled the Monarch of our fashioning,
Who quavered, sank; and now has ceased to be.

X

"So, toward our myth's oblivion,
Darkling, and languid-lipped, we creep and grope
Sadlier than those who wept in Babylon,
Whose Zion was a still abiding hope.

XI

"How sweet it was in years far hied
To start the wheels of day with trustful prayer,
To lie down liegely at the eventide

And feel a blest assurance he was there!

XII

"And who or what shall fill his place?
Whither will wanderers turn distracted eyes
For some fixed star to stimulate their pace
Towards the goal of their enterprise?" . . .

XIII

Some in the background then I saw,
Sweet women, youths, men, all incredulous,
Who chimed as one: "This figure is of straw,
This requiem mockery! Still he lives to us!"

XIV

I could not prop their faith: and yet
Many I had known: with all I sympathized;
And though struck speechless, I did not forget
That what was mourned for, I, too, once had prized.

XV

Still, how to bear such loss I deemed
The insistent question for each animate mind,
And gazing, to my growing sight there seemed
A pale yet positive gleam low down behind,

XVI

   Whereof to lift the general night,
A certain few who stood aloof had said,
"See you upon the horizon that small light -
Swelling somewhat?" Each mourner shook his head.

XVII

   And they composed a crowd of whom
Some were right good, and many nigh the best . . .
Thus dazed and puzzled 'twixt the gleam and gloom
Mechanically I followed with the rest.

1908-10.

SPECTRES THAT GRIEVE

"It is not death that harrows us," they lipped,
"The soundless cell is in itself relief,
For life is an unfenced flower, benumbed and nipped
At unawares, and at its best but brief."

The speakers, sundry phantoms of the gone,
Had risen like filmy flames of phosphor dye,
As if the palest of sheet lightnings shone
From the sward near me, as from a nether sky.

And much surprised was I that, spent and dead,
They should not, like the many, be at rest,

But stray as apparitions; hence I said,
"Why, having slipped life, hark you back distressed?

"We are among the few death sets not free,
The hurt, misrepresented names, who come
At each year's brink, and cry to History
To do them justice, or go past them dumb.

"We are stript of rights; our shames lie unredressed,
Our deeds in full anatomy are not shown,
Our words in morsels merely are expressed
On the scriptured page, our motives blurred, unknown."

Then all these shaken slighted visitants sped
Into the vague, and left me musing there
On fames that well might instance what they had said,
Until the New-Year's dawn strode up the air.

"AH, ARE YOU DIGGING ON MY GRAVE?"

"Ah, are you digging on my grave
    My loved one?--planting rue?"
- "No: yesterday he went to wed
One of the brightest wealth has bred.
'It cannot hurt her now,' he said,
    'That I should not be true.'"

"Then who is digging on my grave?
    My nearest dearest kin?"
- "Ah, no; they sit and think, 'What use!

What good will planting flowers produce?
No tendance of her mound can loose
　　Her spirit from Death's gin.'"

"But some one digs upon my grave?
　　My enemy?--prodding sly?"
- "Nay: when she heard you had passed the Gate
That shuts on all flesh soon or late,
She thought you no more worth her hate,
　　And cares not where you lie."

"Then, who is digging on my grave?
　　Say--since I have not guessed!"
- "O it is I, my mistress dear,
Your little dog, who still lives near,
And much I hope my movements here
　　Have not disturbed your rest?"

"Ah, yes! YOU dig upon my grave . . .
　　Why flashed it not on me
That one true heart was left behind!
What feeling do we ever find
To equal among human kind
　　A dog's fidelity!"

"Mistress, I dug upon your grave
　　To bury a bone, in case
I should be hungry near this spot
When passing on my daily trot.
I am sorry, but I quite forgot
　　It was your resting-place."

SATIRES OF CIRCUMSTANCES
IN FIFTEEN GLIMPSES

I--AT TEA

The kettle descants in a cozy drone,
And the young wife looks in her husband's face,
And then at her guest's, and shows in her own
Her sense that she fills an envied place;
And the visiting lady is all abloom,
And says there was never so sweet a room.

And the happy young housewife does not know
That the woman beside her was first his choice,
Till the fates ordained it could not be so . . .
Betraying nothing in look or voice
The guest sits smiling and sips her tea,
And he throws her a stray glance yearningly.

II--IN CHURCH

"And now to God the Father," he ends,
And his voice thrills up to the topmost tiles:
Each listener chokes as he bows and bends,

And emotion pervades the crowded aisles.
Then the preacher glides to the vestry-door,
And shuts it, and thinks he is seen no more.

The door swings softly ajar meanwhile,
And a pupil of his in the Bible class,
Who adores him as one without gloss or guile,
Sees her idol stand with a satisfied smile
And re-enact at the vestry-glass
Each pulpit gesture in deft dumb-show
That had moved the congregation so.

III--BY HER AUNT'S GRAVE

"Sixpence a week," says the girl to her lover,
"Aunt used to bring me, for she could confide
In me alone, she vowed. 'Twas to cover
The cost of her headstone when she died.
And that was a year ago last June;
I've not yet fixed it. But I must soon."

"And where is the money now, my dear?"
"O, snug in my purse . . . Aunt was SO slow
In saving it--eighty weeks, or near." . . .
"Let's spend it," he hints. "For she won't know.
There's a dance to-night at the Load of Hay."
She passively nods. And they go that way.

IV--IN THE ROOM OF THE BRIDE-ELECT

"Would it had been the man of our wish!"
Sighs her mother. To whom with vehemence she
In the wedding-dress--the wife to be -
"Then why were you so mollyish
As not to insist on him for me!"
The mother, amazed: "Why, dearest one,
Because you pleaded for this or none!"

"But Father and you should have stood out strong!
Since then, to my cost, I have lived to find
That you were right and that I was wrong;
This man is a dolt to the one declined . . .
Ah!--here he comes with his button-hole rose.
Good God--I must marry him I suppose!"

V--AT A WATERING-PLACE

They sit and smoke on the esplanade,
The man and his friend, and regard the bay
Where the far chalk cliffs, to the left displayed,
Smile sallowly in the decline of day.
And saunterers pass with laugh and jest -
A handsome couple among the rest.

"That smart proud pair," says the man to his friend,
"Are to marry next week . . . How little he thinks

That dozens of days and nights on end
I have stroked her neck, unhooked the links
Of her sleeve to get at her upper arm . . .
Well, bliss is in ignorance: what's the harm!"

VI --IN THE CEMETERY

"You see those mothers squabbling there?"
Remarks the man of the cemetery.
One says in tears, "Tis mine lies here!'
Another, 'Nay, mine, you Pharisee!'
Another, 'How dare you move my flowers
And put your own on this grave of ours!'
But all their children were laid therein
At different times, like sprats in a tin.

"And then the main drain had to cross,
And we moved the lot some nights ago,
And packed them away in the general foss
With hundreds more. But their folks don't know,
And as well cry over a new-laid drain
As anything else, to ease your pain!"

VII--OUTSIDE THE WINDOW

"My stick!" he says, and turns in the lane
To the house just left, whence a vixen voice

Comes out with the firelight through the pane,
And he sees within that the girl of his choice
Stands rating her mother with eyes aglare
For something said while he was there.

"At last I behold her soul undraped!"
Thinks the man who had loved her more than himself;
"My God--'tis but narrowly I have escaped. -
My precious porcelain proves it delf."
His face has reddened like one ashamed,
And he steals off, leaving his stick unclaimed.

VIII--IN THE STUDY

He enters, and mute on the edge of a chair
Sits a thin-faced lady, a stranger there,
A type of decayed gentility;
And by some small signs he well can guess
That she comes to him almost breakfastless.

"I have called--I hope I do not err -
I am looking for a purchaser
Of some score volumes of the works
Of eminent divines I own, -
Left by my father--though it irks
My patience to offer them." And she smiles
As if necessity were unknown;
"But the truth of it is that oftenwhiles
I have wished, as I am fond of art,
To make my rooms a little smart."

And lightly still she laughs to him,
As if to sell were a mere gay whim,
And that, to be frank, Life were indeed
To her not vinegar and gall,
But fresh and honey-like; and Need
No household skeleton at all.

IX--AT THE ALTAR-RAIL

"My bride is not coming, alas!" says the groom,
And the telegram shakes in his hand. "I own
It was hurried! We met at a dancing-room
When I went to the Cattle-Show alone,
And then, next night, where the Fountain leaps,
And the Street of the Quarter-Circle sweeps.

"Ay, she won me to ask her to be my wife -
'Twas foolish perhaps!--to forsake the ways
Of the flaring town for a farmer's life.
She agreed. And we fixed it. Now she says:
'It's sweet of you, dear, to prepare me a nest,
But a swift, short, gay life suits me best.
What I really am you have never gleaned;
I had eaten the apple ere you were weaned.'"

X--IN THE NUPTIAL CHAMBER

"O that mastering tune?" And up in the bed
Like a lace-robed phantom springs the bride;
"And why?" asks the man she had that day wed,
With a start, as the band plays on outside.
"It's the townsfolks' cheery compliment
Because of our marriage, my Innocent."

"O but you don't know! 'Tis the passionate air
To which my old Love waltzed with me,
And I swore as we spun that none should share
My home, my kisses, till death, save he!
And he dominates me and thrills me through,
And it's he I embrace while embracing you!"

XI--IN THE RESTAURANT

"But hear. If you stay, and the child be born,
It will pass as your husband's with the rest,
While, if we fly, the teeth of scorn
Will be gleaming at us from east to west;
And the child will come as a life despised;
I feel an elopement is ill-advised!"

"O you realize not what it is, my dear,
To a woman! Daily and hourly alarms
Lest the truth should out. How can I stay here,

And nightly take him into my arms!
Come to the child no name or fame,
Let us go, and face it, and bear the shame."

XII--AT THE DRAPER'S

"I stood at the back of the shop, my dear,
    But you did not perceive me.
Well, when they deliver what you were shown
    _I_ shall know nothing of it, believe me!"

And he coughed and coughed as she paled and said,
    "O, I didn't see you come in there -
Why couldn't you speak?"--"Well, I didn't. I left
    That you should not notice I'd been there.

"You were viewing some lovely things. 'Soon required
    For a widow, of latest fashion';
And I knew 'twould upset you to meet the man
    Who had to be cold and ashen

"And screwed in a box before they could dress you
    'In the last new note in mourning,'
As they defined it. So, not to distress you,
    I left you to your adorning."

XIII--ON THE DEATH-BED

"I'll tell--being past all praying for -
Then promptly die . . . He was out at the war,
And got some scent of the intimacy
That was under way between her and me;
And he stole back home, and appeared like a ghost
One night, at the very time almost
That I reached her house. Well, I shot him dead,
And secretly buried him. Nothing was said.

"The news of the battle came next day;
He was scheduled missing. I hurried away,
Got out there, visited the field,
And sent home word that a search revealed
He was one of the slain; though, lying alone
  And stript, his body had not been known.

"But she suspected. I lost her love,
  Yea, my hope of earth, and of Heaven above;
And my time's now come, and I'll pay the score,
Though it be burning for evermore."

XIV--OVER THE COFFIN

They stand confronting, the coffin between,
His wife of old, and his wife of late,
And the dead man whose they both had been

Seems listening aloof, as to things past date.
--"I have called," says the first. "Do you marvel or not?"
"In truth," says the second, "I do--somewhat."

"Well, there was a word to be said by me! . . .
I divorced that man because of you -
It seemed I must do it, boundenly;
But now I am older, and tell you true,
For life is little, and dead lies he;
I would I had let alone you two!
And both of us, scorning parochial ways,
Had lived like the wives in the patriarchs' days."

XV--IN THE MOONLIGHT

"O lonely workman, standing there
In a dream, why do you stare and stare
At her grave, as no other grave there were?

"If your great gaunt eyes so importune
Her soul by the shine of this corpse-cold moon,
Maybe you'll raise her phantom soon!"

"Why, fool, it is what I would rather see
Than all the living folk there be;
But alas, there is no such joy for me!"

"Ah--she was one you loved, no doubt,
Through good and evil, through rain and drought,
And when she passed, all your sun went out?"

"Nay: she was the woman I did not love,
Whom all the others were ranked above,
Whom during her life I thought nothing of."

SELF-UNCONSCIOUS

Along the way
He walked that day,
Watching shapes that reveries limn,
And seldom he
Had eyes to see
The moment that encompassed him.

Bright yellowhammers
Made mirthful clamours,
And billed long straws with a bustling air,
And bearing their load
Flew up the road
That he followed, alone, without interest there.

From bank to ground
And over and round
They sidled along the adjoining hedge;
Sometimes to the gutter
Their yellow flutter
Would dip from the nearest slatestone ledge.
The smooth sea-line

With a metal shine,
And flashes of white, and a sail thereon,
　　He would also descry
　　With a half-wrapt eye
Between the projects he mused upon.

　Yes, round him were these
　Earth's artistries,
But specious plans that came to his call
　Did most engage
　His pilgrimage,
While himself he did not see at all.

　Dead now as sherds
　Are the yellow birds,
And all that mattered has passed away;
　Yet God, the Elf,
　Now shows him that self
As he was, and should have been shown, that day.

　O it would have been good
　Could he then have stood
At a focussed distance, and conned the whole,
　But now such vision
　Is mere derision,
Nor soothes his body nor saves his soul.

　Not much, some may
　Incline to say,
To see therein, had it all been seen.
　Nay! he is aware
　A thing was there
That loomed with an immortal mien.

THE DISCOVERY

I wandered to a crude coast
  Like a ghost;
Upon the hills I saw fires -
  Funeral pyres
Seemingly--and heard breaking
Waves like distant cannonades that set the land shaking.

And so I never once guessed
  A Love-nest,
Bowered and candle-lit, lay
  In my way,
Till I found a hid hollow,
Where I burst on her my heart could not but follow.

TOLERANCE

"It is a foolish thing," said I,
"To bear with such, and pass it by;
Yet so I do, I know not why!"

And at each clash I would surmise
That if I had acted otherwise
I might have saved me many sighs.

But now the only happiness
In looking back that I possess -
Whose lack would leave me comfortless -

Is to remember I refrained
From masteries I might have gained,
And for my tolerance was disdained;

For see, a tomb. And if it were
I had bent and broke, I should not dare
To linger in the shadows there.

BEFORE AND AFTER SUMMER

I

Looking forward to the spring
One puts up with anything.
On this February day,
Though the winds leap down the street,
Wintry scourgings seem but play,
And these later shafts of sleet
--Sharper pointed than the first -
And these later snows--the worst -
Are as a half-transparent blind
Riddled by rays from sun behind.

II

Shadows of the October pine
Reach into this room of mine:
On the pine there stands a bird;
He is shadowed with the tree.
Mutely perched he bills no word;
Blank as I am even is he.
For those happy suns are past,
Fore-discerned in winter last.
When went by their pleasure, then?
I, alas, perceived not when.

AT DAY-CLOSE IN NOVEMBER

The ten hours' light is abating,
  And a late bird flies across,
Where the pines, like waltzers waiting,
  Give their black heads a toss.

Beech leaves, that yellow the noon-time,
  Float past like specks in the eye;
I set every tree in my June time,
  And now they obscure the sky.

And the children who ramble through here
  Conceive that there never has been
A time when no tall trees grew here,
  A time when none will be seen.

THE YEAR'S AWAKENING

How do you know that the pilgrim track
Along the belting zodiac
Swept by the sun in his seeming rounds
Is traced by now to the Fishes' bounds
And into the Ram, when weeks of cloud
Have wrapt the sky in a clammy shroud,
And never as yet a tint of spring
Has shown in the Earth's apparelling;
  O vespering bird, how do you know,
    How do you know?

How do you know, deep underground,
Hid in your bed from sight and sound,
Without a turn in temperature,
With weather life can scarce endure,
That light has won a fraction's strength,
And day put on some moments' length,
Whereof in merest rote will come,
Weeks hence, mild airs that do not numb;
  O crocus root, how do you know,
    How do you know?

February 1910.

UNDER THE WATERFALL

"Whenever I plunge my arm, like this,
In a basin of water, I never miss
The sweet sharp sense of a fugitive day
Fetched back from its thickening shroud of gray.
   Hence the only prime
   And real love-rhyme
   That I know by heart,
   And that leaves no smart,
Is the purl of a little valley fall
About three spans wide and two spans tall
Over a table of solid rock,
And into a scoop of the self-same block;
The purl of a runlet that never ceases
In stir of kingdoms, in wars, in peaces;
With a hollow boiling voice it speaks
And has spoken since hills were turfless peaks."

"And why gives this the only prime
Idea to you of a real love-rhyme?
And why does plunging your arm in a bowl
Full of spring water, bring throbs to your soul?
Well, under the fall, in a crease of the stone,
Though where precisely none ever has known,
Jammed darkly, nothing to show how prized,
And by now with its smoothness opalized,
   Is a drinking-glass:
   For, down that pass
   My lover and I
   Walked under a sky

Of blue with a leaf-woven awning of green,
In the burn of August, to paint the scene,
And we placed our basket of fruit and wine
By the runlet's rim, where we sat to dine;
And when we had drunk from the glass together,
Arched by the oak-copse from the weather,
I held the vessel to rinse in the fall,
Where it slipped, and sank, and was past recall,
Though we stooped and plumbed the little abyss
With long bared arms. There the glass still is.
And, as said, if I thrust my arm below
Cold water in basin or bowl, a throe
From the past awakens a sense of that time,
And the glass both used, and the cascade's rhyme.
The basin seems the pool, and its edge
The hard smooth face of the brook-side ledge,
And the leafy pattern of china-ware
The hanging plants that were bathing there.
By night, by day, when it shines or lours,
There lies intact that chalice of ours,
And its presence adds to the rhyme of love
Persistently sung by the fall above.
No lip has touched it since his and mine
In turns therefrom sipped lovers' wine."

THE SPELL OF THE ROSE

"I mean to build a hall anon,
　And shape two turrets there,
　And a broad newelled stair,
And a cool well for crystal water;
　Yes; I will build a hall anon,
　Plant roses love shall feed upon,
　And apple trees and pear."

He set to build the manor-hall,
　And shaped the turrets there,
　And the broad newelled stair,
And the cool well for crystal water;
　He built for me that manor-hall,
　And planted many trees withal,
　But no rose anywhere.

And as he planted never a rose
　That bears the flower of love,
　Though other flowers throve
A frost-wind moved our souls to sever
　Since he had planted never a rose;
　And misconceits raised horrid shows,
　And agonies came thereof.

"I'll mend these miseries," then said I,
　And so, at dead of night,
　I went and, screened from sight,
That nought should keep our souls in severance,
　I set a rose-bush. "This," said I,

"May end divisions dire and wry,
  And long-drawn days of blight."

But I was called from earth--yea, called
  Before my rose-bush grew;
  And would that now I knew
What feels he of the tree I planted,
  And whether, after I was called
  To be a ghost, he, as of old,
    Gave me his heart anew!

Perhaps now blooms that queen of trees
  I set but saw not grow,
  And he, beside its glow -
Eyes couched of the mis-vision that blurred me -
  Ay, there beside that queen of trees
  He sees me as I was, though sees
    Too late to tell me so!

ST. LAUNCE'S REVISITED

  Slip back, Time!
Yet again I am nearing
Castle and keep, uprearing
  Gray, as in my prime.

  At the inn
Smiling close, why is it
Not as on my visit
  When hope and I were twin?

Groom and jade
Whom I found here, moulder;
Strange the tavern-holder,
　Strange the tap-maid.

　Here I hired
Horse and man for bearing
Me on my wayfaring
　To the door desired.

　Evening gloomed
As I journeyed forward
To the faces shoreward,
　Till their dwelling loomed.

　If again
Towards the Atlantic sea there
I should speed, they'd be there
　Surely now as then? . . .

　Why waste thought,
When I know them vanished
Under earth; yea, banished
　Ever into nought.

POEMS OF 1912-13
Veteris vestigia flammae

THE GOING

Why did you give no hint that night
That quickly after the morrow's dawn,
And calmly, as if indifferent quite,
You would close your term here, up and be gone
　　Where I could not follow
　　With wing of swallow
To gain one glimpse of you ever anon!

　　Never to bid good-bye,
　　Or give me the softest call,
Or utter a wish for a word, while I
Saw morning harden upon the wall,
　　Unmoved, unknowing
　　That your great going
Had place that moment, and altered all.

Why do you make me leave the house
And think for a breath it is you I see

At the end of the alley of bending boughs
Where so often at dusk you used to be;
  Till in darkening dankness
  The yawning blankness
Of the perspective sickens me!

  You were she who abode
  By those red-veined rocks far West,
You were the swan-necked one who rode
Along the beetling Beeny Crest,
  And, reining nigh me,
  Would muse and eye me,
While Life unrolled us its very best.

Why, then, latterly did we not speak,
Did we not think of those days long dead,
And ere your vanishing strive to seek
That time's renewal? We might have said,
  "In this bright spring weather
  We'll visit together
Those places that once we visited."

  Well, well! All's past amend,
  Unchangeable. It must go.
I seem but a dead man held on end
To sink down soon . . . O you could not know
  That such swift fleeing
  No soul foreseeing -
Not even I--would undo me so!

December 1912.

YOUR LAST DRIVE

Here by the moorway you returned,
And saw the borough lights ahead
That lit your face--all undiscerned
To be in a week the face of the dead,
And you told of the charm of that haloed view
That never again would beam on you.

And on your left you passed the spot
Where eight days later you were to lie,
And be spoken of as one who was not;
Beholding it with a cursory eye
As alien from you, though under its tree
You soon would halt everlastingly.

I drove not with you . . . Yet had I sat
At your side that eve I should not have seen
That the countenance I was glancing at
Had a last-time look in the flickering sheen,
Nor have read the writing upon your face,
"I go hence soon to my resting-place;

"You may miss me then. But I shall not know
How many times you visit me there,
Or what your thoughts are, or if you go
There never at all. And I shall not care.
Should you censure me I shall take no heed
And even your praises I shall not need."

True: never you'll know. And you will not mind.
But shall I then slight you because of such?
Dear ghost, in the past did you ever find
The thought "What profit?" move me much
Yet the fact indeed remains the same,
You are past love, praise, indifference, blame.

December 1912.

THE WALK

   You did not walk with me
   Of late to the hill-top tree
      By the gated ways,
      As in earlier days;
      You were weak and lame,
      So you never came,
And I went alone, and I did not mind,
Not thinking of you as left behind.

   I walked up there to-day
   Just in the former way:
      Surveyed around
      The familiar ground
      By myself again:
      What difference, then?
Only that underlying sense
Of the look of a room on returning thence.

RAIN ON A GRAVE

Clouds spout upon her
  Their waters amain
  In ruthless disdain, -
Her who but lately
  Had shivered with pain
As at touch of dishonour
If there had lit on her
So coldly, so straightly
  Such arrows of rain.

She who to shelter
  Her delicate head
Would quicken and quicken
  Each tentative tread
If drops chanced to pelt her
  That summertime spills
  In dust-paven rills
When thunder-clouds thicken
  And birds close their bills.

Would that I lay there
  And she were housed here!
Or better, together
Were folded away there
Exposed to one weather
We both,--who would stray there
When sunny the day there,
  Or evening was clear
  At the prime of the year.

Soon will be growing
    Green blades from her mound,
And daises be showing
    Like stars on the ground,
Till she form part of them -
Ay--the sweet heart of them,
Loved beyond measure
With a child's pleasure
    All her life's round.

Jan. 31, 1913.

"I FOUND HER OUT THERE"

I found her out there
On a slope few see,
That falls westwardly
To the salt-edged air,
Where the ocean breaks
On the purple strand,
And the hurricane shakes
The solid land.

I brought her here,
And have laid her to rest
In a noiseless nest
No sea beats near.
She will never be stirred
In her loamy cell
By the waves long heard

And loved so well.

So she does not sleep
By those haunted heights
The Atlantic smites
And the blind gales sweep,
Whence she often would gaze
At Dundagel's far head,
While the dipping blaze
Dyed her face fire-red;

And would sigh at the tale
Of sunk Lyonnesse,
As a wind-tugged tress
Flapped her cheek like a flail;
Or listen at whiles
With a thought-bound brow
To the murmuring miles
She is far from now.

Yet her shade, maybe,
Will creep underground
Till it catch the sound
Of that western sea
As it swells and sobs
Where she once domiciled,
And joy in its throbs
With the heart of a child.

WITHOUT CEREMONY

It was your way, my dear,
To be gone without a word
When callers, friends, or kin
Had left, and I hastened in
To rejoin you, as I inferred.

And when you'd a mind to career
Off anywhere--say to town -
You were all on a sudden gone
Before I had thought thereon,
Or noticed your trunks were down.

So, now that you disappear
For ever in that swift style,
Your meaning seems to me
Just as it used to be:
"Good-bye is not worth while!"

LAMENT

How she would have loved
A party to-day! -
Bright-hatted and gloved,
With table and tray
And chairs on the lawn

Her smiles would have shone
With welcomings . . . But
She is shut, she is shut
　From friendship's spell
　In the jailing shell
　Of her tiny cell.

Or she would have reigned
At a dinner to-night
With ardours unfeigned,
And a generous delight;
All in her abode
She'd have freely bestowed
On her guests . . . But alas,
She is shut under grass
　Where no cups flow,
　Powerless to know
　That it might be so.

And she would have sought
With a child's eager glance
The shy snowdrops brought
By the new year's advance,
And peered in the rime
Of Candlemas-time
For crocuses . . . chanced
It that she were not tranced
　From sights she loved best;
　Wholly possessed
　By an infinite rest!

And we are here staying
Amid these stale things

Who care not for gaying,
And those junketings
That used so to joy her,
And never to cloy her
As us they cloy! . . . But
She is shut, she is shut
From the cheer of them, dead
To all done and said
In a yew-arched bed.

THE HAUNTER

He does not think that I haunt here nightly:
  How shall I let him know
That whither his fancy sets him wandering
  I, too, alertly go? -
Hover and hover a few feet from him
  Just as I used to do,
But cannot answer his words addressed me -
  Only listen thereto!

When I could answer he did not say them:
  When I could let him know
How I would like to join in his journeys
  Seldom he wished to go.
Now that he goes and wants me with him
  More than he used to do,
Never he sees my faithful phantom
  Though he speaks thereto.

Yes, I accompany him to places
  Only dreamers know,
Where the shy hares limp long paces,
  Where the night rooks go;
Into old aisles where the past is all to him,
  Close as his shade can do,
Always lacking the power to call to him,
  Near as I reach thereto!

What a good haunter I am, O tell him,
  Quickly make him know
If he but sigh since my loss befell him
  Straight to his side I go.
Tell him a faithful one is doing
  All that love can do
Still that his path may be worth pursuing,
  And to bring peace thereto.

THE VOICE

Woman much missed, how you call to me, call to me,
Saying that now you are not as you were
When you had changed from the one who was all to me,
But as at first, when our day was fair.

Can it be you that I hear? Let me view you, then,
Standing as when I drew near to the town
Where you would wait for me: yes, as I knew you then,
Even to the original air-blue gown!

Or is it only the breeze, in its listlessness
Travelling across the wet mead to me here,
You being ever consigned to existlessness,
Heard no more again far or near?

  Thus I; faltering forward,
  Leaves around me falling,
Wind oozing thin through the thorn from norward
  And the woman calling.

December 1912.

HIS VISITOR

I come across from Mellstock while the moon wastes weaker
To behold where I lived with you for twenty years and more:
I shall go in the gray, at the passing of the mail-train,
And need no setting open of the long familiar door
  As before.

The change I notice in my once own quarters!
A brilliant budded border where the daisies used to be,
The rooms new painted, and the pictures altered,
And other cups and saucers, and no cozy nook for tea
  As with me.

I discern the dim faces of the sleep-wrapt servants;
They are not those who tended me through feeble hours and strong,
But strangers quite, who never knew my rule here,
Who never saw me painting, never heard my softling song

Float along.

So I don't want to linger in this re-decked dwelling,
I feel too uneasy at the contrasts I behold,
And I make again for Mellstock to return here never,
And rejoin the roomy silence, and the mute and manifold
  Souls of old.

1913.

A CIRCULAR

As "legal representative"
I read a missive not my own,
On new designs the senders give
  For clothes, in tints as shown.

Here figure blouses, gowns for tea,
And presentation-trains of state,
Charming ball-dresses, millinery,
  Warranted up to date.

And this gay-pictured, spring-time shout
Of Fashion, hails what lady proud?
Her who before last year was out
  Was costumed in a shroud.

A DREAM OR NO

Why go to Saint-Juliot? What's Juliot to me?
  I was but made fancy
  By some necromancy
That much of my life claims the spot as its key.

Yes. I have had dreams of that place in the West,
  And a maiden abiding
  Thereat as in hiding;
Fair-eyed and white-shouldered, broad-browed and brown-tressed.

And of how, coastward bound on a night long ago,
  There lonely I found her,
  The sea-birds around her,
And other than nigh things uncaring to know.

So sweet her life there (in my thought has it seemed)
  That quickly she drew me
  To take her unto me,
And lodge her long years with me. Such have I dreamed.

But nought of that maid from Saint-Juliot I see;
  Can she ever have been here,
  And shed her life's sheen here,
The woman I thought a long housemate with me?

Does there even a place like Saint-Juliot exist?
  Or a Vallency Valley
  With stream and leafed alley,
Or Beeny, or Bos with its flounce flinging mist?

AFTER A JOURNEY

Hereto I come to interview a ghost;
　Whither, O whither will its whim now draw me?
Up the cliff, down, till I'm lonely, lost,
　And the unseen waters' ejaculations awe me.
Where you will next be there's no knowing,
　Facing round about me everywhere,
　　With your nut-coloured hair,
And gray eyes, and rose-flush coming and going.

Yes: I have re-entered your olden haunts at last;
　Through the years, through the dead scenes I have tracked you;
What have you now found to say of our past -
　Viewed across the dark space wherein I have lacked you?
Summer gave us sweets, but autumn wrought division?
　Things were not lastly as firstly well
　　With us twain, you tell?
But all's closed now, despite Time's derision.

I see what you are doing: you are leading me on
　To the spots we knew when we haunted here together,
The waterfall, above which the mist-bow shone
　At the then fair hour in the then fair weather,
And the cave just under, with a voice still so hollow
　That it seems to call out to me from forty years ago,
　　When you were all aglow,
And not the thin ghost that I now frailly follow!

Ignorant of what there is flitting here to see,
　The waked birds preen and the seals flop lazily,

Soon you will have, Dear, to vanish from me,
  For the stars close their shutters and the dawn whitens hazily.
Trust me, I mind not, though Life lours,
  The bringing me here; nay, bring me here again!
    I am just the same as when
Our days were a joy, and our paths through flowers.

PENTARGAN BAY.

A DEATH-DAY RECALLED

Beeny did not quiver,
  Juliot grew not gray,
Thin Valency's river
  Held its wonted way.
Bos seemed not to utter
  Dimmest note of dirge,
Targan mouth a mutter
  To its creamy surge.

Yet though these, unheeding,
  Listless, passed the hour
Of her spirit's speeding,
  She had, in her flower,
Sought and loved the places -
  Much and often pined
For their lonely faces
  When in towns confined.

Why did not Valency
  In his purl deplore
One whose haunts were whence he
  Drew his limpid store?
Why did Bos not thunder,
  Targan apprehend
Body and breath were sunder
  Of their former friend?

BEENY CLIFF
March 1870--March 1913

I

O the opal and the sapphire of that wandering western sea,
And the woman riding high above with bright hair flapping free -
The woman whom I loved so, and who loyally loved me.

II

The pale mews plained below us, and the waves seemed far away
In a nether sky, engrossed in saying their ceaseless babbling say,
As we laughed light-heartedly aloft on that clear-sunned March day.

III

A little cloud then cloaked us, and there flew an irised rain,
And the Atlantic dyed its levels with a dull misfeatured stain,
And then the sun burst out again, and purples prinked the main.

IV

--Still in all its chasmal beauty bulks old Beeny to the sky,
And shall she and I not go there once again now March is nigh,
And the sweet things said in that March say anew there by and by?

V

What if still in chasmal beauty looms that wild weird western shore,
The woman now is--elsewhere--whom the ambling pony bore,
And nor knows nor cares for Beeny, and will see it nevermore.

AT CASTLE BOTEREL

As I drive to the junction of lane and highway,
  And the drizzle bedrenches the waggonette,
I look behind at the fading byway,
  And see on its slope, now glistening wet,
    Distinctly yet

Myself and a girlish form benighted
  In dry March weather. We climb the road
Beside a chaise. We had just alighted
  To ease the sturdy pony's load
    When he sighed and slowed.

What we did as we climbed, and what we talked of
  Matters not much, nor to what it led, -
Something that life will not be balked of
  Without rude reason till hope is dead,

And feeling fled.

It filled but a minute. But was there ever
  A time of such quality, since or before,
In that hill's story? To one mind never,
  Though it has been climbed, foot-swift, foot-sore,
    By thousands more.

Primaeval rocks form the road's steep border,
  And much have they faced there, first and last,
Of the transitory in Earth's long order;
  But what they record in colour and cast
    Is--that we two passed.

And to me, though Time's unflinching rigour,
  In mindless rote, has ruled from sight
The substance now, one phantom figure
  Remains on the slope, as when that night
    Saw us alight.

I look and see it there, shrinking, shrinking,
  I look back at it amid the rain
For the very last time; for my sand is sinking,
  And I shall traverse old love's domain
    Never again.

March 1913.

PLACES

Nobody says: Ah, that is the place
Where chanced, in the hollow of years ago,
What none of the Three Towns cared to know--
The birth of a little girl of grace -
The sweetest the house saw, first or last;
   Yet it was so
   On that day long past.

Nobody thinks: There, there she lay
In a room by the Hoe, like the bud of a flower,
And listened, just after the bedtime hour,
To the stammering chimes that used to play
The quaint Old Hundred-and-Thirteenth tune
   In Saint Andrew's tower
   Night, morn, and noon.

Nobody calls to mind that here
Upon Boterel Hill, where the carters skid,
With cheeks whose airy flush outbid
Fresh fruit in bloom, and free of fear,
She cantered down, as if she must fall
   (Though she never did),
   To the charm of all.

Nay: one there is to whom these things,
That nobody else's mind calls back,
Have a savour that scenes in being lack,
And a presence more than the actual brings;
To whom to-day is beneaped and stale,

And its urgent clack
But a vapid tale.

PLYMOUTH, March 1913.

THE PHANTOM HORSEWOMAN

I

Queer are the ways of a man I know:
  He comes and stands
  In a careworn craze,
  And looks at the sands
  And the seaward haze,
  With moveless hands
  And face and gaze,
  Then turns to go . . .
And what does he see when he gazes so?

II

They say he sees as an instant thing
  More clear than to-day,
  A sweet soft scene
  That once was in play
  By that briny green;
  Yes, notes alway
  Warm, real, and keen,
  What his back years bring -
A phantom of his own figuring.

III

Of this vision of his they might say more:
  Not only there
  Does he see this sight,
  But everywhere
  In his brain--day, night,
  As if on the air
  It were drawn rose bright -
  Yea, far from that shore
Does he carry this vision of heretofore:

IV

A ghost-girl-rider. And though, toil-tried,
  He withers daily,
  Time touches her not,
  But she still rides gaily
  In his rapt thought
  On that shagged and shaly
  Atlantic spot,
  And as when first eyed
Draws rein and sings to the swing of the tide.

MISCELLANEOUS PIECES

THE WISTFUL LADY

'Love, while you were away there came to me -
 From whence I cannot tell -
A plaintive lady pale and passionless,
Who bent her eyes upon me critically,
And weighed me with a wearing wistfulness,
 As if she knew me well."

"I saw no lady of that wistful sort
 As I came riding home.
Perhaps she was some dame the Fates constrain
By memories sadder than she can support,
Or by unhappy vacancy of brain,
 To leave her roof and roam?"

"Ah, but she knew me. And before this time
 I have seen her, lending ear
To my light outdoor words, and pondering each,
Her frail white finger swayed in pantomime,
As if she fain would close with me in speech,
 And yet would not come near.

"And once I saw her beckoning with her hand
  As I came into sight
At an upper window. And I at last went out;
But when I reached where she had seemed to stand,
And wandered up and down and searched about,
  I found she had vanished quite."

Then thought I how my dead Love used to say,
  With a small smile, when she
Was waning wan, that she would hover round
And show herself after her passing day
To any newer Love I might have found,
  But show her not to me.

THE WOMAN IN THE RYE

"Why do you stand in the dripping rye,
Cold-lipped, unconscious, wet to the knee,
When there are firesides near?" said I.
"I told him I wished him dead," said she.

"Yea, cried it in my haste to one
Whom I had loved, whom I well loved still;
And die he did. And I hate the sun,
And stand here lonely, aching, chill;

"Stand waiting, waiting under skies
That blow reproach, the while I see
The rooks sheer off to where he lies
Wrapt in a peace withheld from me."

THE CHEVAL-GLASS

Why do you harbour that great cheval-glass
  Filling up your narrow room?
  You never preen or plume,
Or look in a week at your full-length figure -
  Picture of bachelor gloom!

"Well, when I dwelt in ancient England,
  Renting the valley farm,
  Thoughtless of all heart-harm,
I used to gaze at the parson's daughter,
  A creature of nameless charm.

"Thither there came a lover and won her,
  Carried her off from my view.
  O it was then I knew
Misery of a cast undreamt of -
  More than, indeed, my due!

"Then far rumours of her ill-usage
  Came, like a chilling breath
  When a man languisheth;
Followed by news that her mind lost balance,
  And, in a space, of her death.

"Soon sank her father; and next was the auction -
  Everything to be sold:
  Mid things new and old
Stood this glass in her former chamber,
  Long in her use, I was told.

"Well, I awaited the sale and bought it . . .
 There by my bed it stands,
 And as the dawn expands
Often I see her pale-faced form there
 Brushing her hair's bright bands.

"There, too, at pallid midnight moments
 Quick she will come to my call,
 Smile from the frame withal
Ponderingly, as she used to regard me
 Passing her father's wall.

"So that it was for its revelations
 I brought it oversea,
 And drag it about with me . . .
Anon I shall break it and bury its fragments
 Where my grave is to be."

THE RE-ENACTMENT

Between the folding sea-downs,
 In the gloom
Of a wailful wintry nightfall,
 When the boom
Of the ocean, like a hammering in a hollow tomb,

Throbbed up the copse-clothed valley
 From the shore
To the chamber where I darkled,
 Sunk and sore

With gray ponderings why my Loved one had not come before

  To salute me in the dwelling
    That of late
  I had hired to waste a while in -
    Vague of date,
Quaint, and remote--wherein I now expectant sate;

  On the solitude, unsignalled,
    Broke a man
  Who, in air as if at home there,
    Seemed to scan
Every fire-flecked nook of the apartment span by span.

  A stranger's and no lover's
    Eyes were these,
  Eyes of a man who measures
    What he sees
But vaguely, as if wrapt in filmy phantasies.

  Yea, his bearing was so absent
    As he stood,
  It bespoke a chord so plaintive
    In his mood,
That soon I judged he would not wrong my quietude.

  "Ah--the supper is just ready,"
    Then he said,
  "And the years'-long binned Madeira
    Flashes red!"
(There was no wine, no food, no supper-table spread.)

  "You will forgive my coming,

Lady fair?
I see you as at that time
    Rising there,
The self-same curious querying in your eyes and air.

"Yet no. How so? You wear not
    The same gown,
Your locks show woful difference,
    Are not brown:
What, is it not as when I hither came from town?

"And the place . . . But you seem other -
    Can it be?
What's this that Time is doing
    Unto me?
YOU dwell here, unknown woman? . . . Whereabouts, then, is she?

"And the house--things are much shifted. -
    Put them where
They stood on this night's fellow;
    Shift her chair:
Here was the couch: and the piano should be there."

I indulged him, verily nerve-strained
    Being alone,
And I moved the things as bidden,
    One by one,
And feigned to push the old piano where he had shown.

"Aha--now I can see her!
    Stand aside:
Don't thrust her from the table
    Where, meek-eyed,

She makes attempt with matron-manners to preside.

"She serves me: now she rises,
    Goes to play . . .
But you obstruct her, fill her
    With dismay,
And embarrassed, scared, she vanishes away!"

And, as 'twere useless longer
    To persist,
He sighed, and sought the entry
    Ere I wist,
And retreated, disappearing soundless in the mist.

That here some mighty passion
    Once had burned,
Which still the walls enghosted,
    I discerned,
And that by its strong spell mine might be overturned.

I sat depressed; till, later,
    My Love came;
But something in the chamber
    Dimmed our flame, -
An emanation, making our due words fall tame,

As if the intenser drama
    Shown me there
Of what the walls had witnessed
    Filled the air,
And left no room for later passion anywhere.

So came it that our fervours
   Did quite fail
Of future consummation -
   Being made quail
By the weird witchery of the parlour's hidden tale,

Which I, as years passed, faintly
   Learnt to trace, -
One of sad love, born full-winged
   In that place
Where the predestined sorrowers first stood face to face.

And as that month of winter
   Circles round,
And the evening of the date-day
   Grows embrowned,
I am conscious of those presences, and sit spellbound.

There, often--lone, forsaken -
   Queries breed
Within me; whether a phantom
   Had my heed
On that strange night, or was it some wrecked heart indeed?

HER SECRET

That love's dull smart distressed my heart
   He shrewdly learnt to see,
But that I was in love with a dead man
   Never suspected he.

He searched for the trace of a pictured face,
   He watched each missive come,
And a note that seemed like a love-line
   Made him look frozen and glum.

He dogged my feet to the city street,
   He followed me to the sea,
But not to the neighbouring churchyard
   Did he dream of following me.

"SHE CHARGED ME"

She charged me with having said this and that
To another woman long years before,
In the very parlour where we sat, -

Sat on a night when the endless pour
Of rain on the roof and the road below
Bent the spring of the spirit more and more . . .

- So charged she me; and the Cupid's bow
Of her mouth was hard, and her eyes, and her face,
And her white forefinger lifted slow.

Had she done it gently, or shown a trace
That not too curiously would she view
A folly passed ere her reign had place,

A kiss might have ended it. But I knew
From the fall of each word, and the pause between,
That the curtain would drop upon us two
Ere long, in our play of slave and queen.

THE NEWCOMER'S WIFE

He paused on the sill of a door ajar
That screened a lively liquor-bar,
For the name had reached him through the door
Of her he had married the week before.

"We called her the Hack of the Parade;
But she was discreet in the games she played;
If slightly worn, she's pretty yet,
And gossips, after all, forget.

"And he knows nothing of her past;
I am glad the girl's in luck at last;
Such ones, though stale to native eyes,
Newcomers snatch at as a prize."

"Yes, being a stranger he sees her blent
Of all that's fresh and innocent,
Nor dreams how many a love-campaign
She had enjoyed before his reign!"

That night there was the splash of a fall
Over the slimy harbour-wall:
They searched, and at the deepest place
Found him with crabs upon his face.

A CONVERSATION AT DAWN

He lay awake, with a harassed air,
And she, in her cloud of loose lank hair,
 Seemed trouble-tried
As the dawn drew in on their faces there.

The chamber looked far over the sea
From a white hotel on a white-stoned quay,
 And stepping a stride
He parted the window-drapery.

Above the level horizon spread
The sunrise, firing them foot to head
 From its smouldering lair,
And painting their pillows with dyes of red.

"What strange disquiets have stirred you, dear,
This dragging night, with starts in fear
 Of me, as it were,

Or of something evil hovering near?"

"My husband, can I have fear of you?
What should one fear from a man whom few,
  Or none, had matched
In that late long spell of delays undue!"

He watched her eyes in the heaving sun:
"Then what has kept, O reticent one,
  Those lids unlatched -
Anything promised I've not yet done?"

"O it's not a broken promise of yours
(For what quite lightly your lip assures
  The due time brings)
That has troubled my sleep, and no waking cures!" . . .

"I have shaped my will; 'tis at hand," said he;
"I subscribe it to-day, that no risk there be
  In the hap of things
Of my leaving you menaced by poverty."

"That a boon provision I'm safe to get,
Signed, sealed by my lord as it were a debt,
  I cannot doubt,
Or ever this peering sun be set."

"But you flung my arms away from your side,
And faced the wall. No month-old bride
  Ere the tour be out
In an air so loth can be justified?

"Ah--had you a male friend once loved well,
Upon whose suit disaster fell
    And frustrance swift?
Honest you are, and may care to tell."

She lay impassive, and nothing broke
The stillness other than, stroke by stroke,
    The lazy lift
Of the tide below them; till she spoke:

"I once had a friend--a Love, if you will -
Whose wife forsook him, and sank until
    She was made a thrall
In a prison-cell for a deed of ill . . .

"He remained alone; and we met--to love,
But barring legitimate joy thereof
    Stood a doorless wall,
Though we prized each other all else above.

"And this was why, though I'd touched my prime,
I put off suitors from time to time -
    Yourself with the rest -
Till friends, who approved you, called it crime,

"And when misgivings weighed on me
In my lover's absence, hurriedly,
    And much distrest,
I took you . . . Ah, that such could be! . . .

"Now, saw you when crossing from yonder shore
At yesternoon, that the packet bore
    On a white-wreathed bier

A coffined body towards the fore?

"Well, while you stood at the other end,
The loungers talked, and I could but lend
   A listening ear,
For they named the dead. 'Twas the wife of my friend.

"He was there, but did not note me, veiled,
Yet I saw that a joy, as of one unjailed,
   Now shone in his gaze;
He knew not his hope of me just had failed!

"They had brought her home: she was born in this isle;
And he will return to his domicile,
   And pass his days
Alone, and not as he dreamt erstwhile!"

"--So you've lost a sprucer spouse than I!"
She held her peace, as if fain deny
   She would indeed
For his pleasure's sake, but could lip no lie.

"One far less formal and plain and slow!"
She let the laconic assertion go
   As if of need
She held the conviction that it was so.

"Regard me as his he always should,
He had said, and wed me he vowed he would
   In his prime or sere
Most verily do, if ever he could.

"And this fulfilment is now his aim,
For a letter, addressed in my maiden name,
   Has dogged me here,
Reminding me faithfully of his claim.

"And it started a hope like a lightning-streak
That I might go to him--say for a week -
   And afford you right
To put me away, and your vows unspeak.

"To be sure you have said, as of dim intent,
That marriage is a plain event
   Of black and white,
Without any ghost of sentiment,

"And my heart has quailed.--But deny it true
That you will never this lock undo!
   No God intends
To thwart the yearning He's father to!"

The husband hemmed, then blandly bowed
In the light of the angry morning cloud.
   "So my idyll ends,
And a drama opens!" he mused aloud;

And his features froze. "You may take it as true
That I will never this lock undo
   For so depraved
A passion as that which kindles you."

Said she: "I am sorry you see it so;
I had hoped you might have let me go,
   And thus been saved

The pain of learning there's more to know."

"More? What may that be? Gad, I think
You have told me enough to make me blink!
   Yet if more remain
Then own it to me. I will not shrink!"

"Well, it is this. As we could not see
That a legal marriage could ever be,
   To end our pain
We united ourselves informally;

"And vowed at a chancel-altar nigh,
With book and ring, a lifelong tie;
   A contract vain
To the world, but real to Him on High."

"And you became as his wife?"--"I did." -
He stood as stiff as a caryatid,
   And said, "Indeed! . . .
No matter. You're mine, whatever you ye hid!"

"But is it right! When I only gave
My hand to you in a sweat to save,
   Through desperate need
(As I thought), my fame, for I was not brave!"

"To save your fame? Your meaning is dim,
For nobody knew of your altar-whim?"
   "I mean--I feared
There might be fruit of my tie with him;

"And to cloak it by marriage I'm not the first,
Though, maybe, morally most accurst
   Through your unpeered
And strict uprightness. That's the worst!

"While yesterday his worn contours
Convinced me that love like his endures,
   And that my troth-plight
Had been his, in fact, and not truly yours."

"So, my lady, you raise the veil by degrees . . .
I own this last is enough to freeze
   The warmest wight!
Now hear the other side, if you please:

"I did say once, though without intent,
That marriage is a plain event
   Of black and white,
Whatever may be its sentiment.

"I'll act accordingly, none the less
That you soiled the contract in time of stress,
   Thereto induced
By the feared results of your wantonness.

"But the thing is over, and no one knows,
And it's nought to the future what you disclose.
   That you'll be loosed
For such an episode, don't suppose!

"No: I'll not free you. And if it appear
There was too good ground for your first fear
   From your amorous tricks,

I'll father the child. Yes, by God, my dear.

"Even should you fly to his arms, I'll damn
Opinion, and fetch you; treat as sham
    Your mutinous kicks,
And whip you home. That's the sort I am!"

She whitened. "Enough . . . Since you disapprove
I'll yield in silence, and never move
    Till my last pulse ticks
A footstep from the domestic groove."

"Then swear it," he said, "and your king uncrown."
He drew her forth in her long white gown,
    And she knelt and swore.
"Good. Now you may go and again lie down

"Since you've played these pranks and given no sign,
You shall crave this man of yours; pine and pine
    With sighings sore,
'Till I've starved your love for him; nailed you mine.

"I'm a practical man, and want no tears;
You've made a fool of me, it appears;
    That you don't again
Is a lesson I'll teach you in future years."

She answered not, but lay listlessly
With her dark dry eyes on the coppery sea,
    That now and then
Flung its lazy flounce at the neighbouring quay.

1910.

A KING'S SOLILOQUY
ON THE NIGHT OF HIS FUNERAL

From the slow march and muffled drum
   And crowds distrest,
And book and bell, at length I have come
   To my full rest.

A ten years' rule beneath the sun
   Is wound up here,
And what I have done, what left undone,
   Figures out clear.

Yet in the estimate of such
   It grieves me more
That I by some was loved so much
   Than that I bore,

From others, judgment of that hue
   Which over-hope
Breeds from a theoretic view
   Of regal scope.

For kingly opportunities
   Right many have sighed;
How best to bear its devilries
   Those learn who have tried!

I have eaten the fat and drunk the sweet,

Lived the life out
From the first greeting glad drum-beat
　　To the last shout.

What pleasure earth affords to kings
　　I have enjoyed
Through its long vivid pulse-stirrings
　　Even till it cloyed.

What days of drudgery, nights of stress
　　Can cark a throne,
Even one maintained in peacefulness,
　　I too have known.

And so, I think, could I step back
　　To life again,
I should prefer the average track
　　Of average men,

Since, as with them, what kingship would
　　It cannot do,
Nor to first thoughts however good
　　Hold itself true.

Something binds hard the royal hand,
　　As all that be,
And it is That has shaped, has planned
　　My acts and me.

May 1910.

THE CORONATION

At Westminster, hid from the light of day,
Many who once had shone as monarchs lay.

Edward the Pious, and two Edwards more,
The second Richard, Henrys three or four;

That is to say, those who were called the Third,
Fifth, Seventh, and Eighth (the much self-widowered),

And James the Scot, and near him Charles the Second,
And, too, the second George could there be reckoned.

Of women, Mary and Queen Elizabeth,
And Anne, all silent in a musing death;

And William's Mary, and Mary, Queen of Scots,
And consort-queens whose names oblivion blots;

And several more whose chronicle one sees
Adorning ancient royal pedigrees.

- Now, as they drowsed on, freed from Life's old thrall,
And heedless, save of things exceptional,

Said one: "What means this throbbing thudding sound
That reaches to us here from overground;

"A sound of chisels, augers, planes, and saws,
Infringing all ecclesiastic laws?

"And these tons-weight of timber on us pressed,
Unfelt here since we entered into rest?

"Surely, at least to us, being corpses royal,
A meet repose is owing by the loyal?"

"--Perhaps a scaffold!" Mary Stuart sighed,
"If such still be. It was that way I died."

"--Ods! Far more like," said he the many-wived,
"That for a wedding 'tis this work's contrived.

"Ha-ha! I never would bow down to Rimmon,
But I had a rare time with those six women!"

"Not all at once?" gasped he who loved confession.
"Nay, nay!" said Hal. "That would have been transgression."

"--They build a catafalque here, black and tall,
Perhaps," mused Richard, "for some funeral?"

And Anne chimed in: "Ah, yes: it maybe so!"
"Nay!" squeaked Eliza. "Little you seem to know -

"Clearly 'tis for some crowning here in state,
As they crowned us at our long bygone date;

"Though we'd no such a power of carpentry,
But let the ancient architecture be;

"If I were up there where the parsons sit,
In one of my gold robes, I'd see to it!"

"But you are not," Charles chuckled. "You are here,
And never will know the sun again, my dear!"

"Yea," whispered those whom no one had addressed;
"With slow, sad march, amid a folk distressed,
We were brought here, to take our dusty rest.

"And here, alas, in darkness laid below,
We'll wait and listen, and endure the show . . .
Clamour dogs kingship; afterwards not so!"

1911.

AQUAE SULIS

The chimes called midnight, just at interlune,
And the daytime talk of the Roman investigations
Was checked by silence, save for the husky tune
The bubbling waters played near the excavations.

And a warm air came up from underground,
And a flutter, as of a filmy shape unsepulchred,
That collected itself, and waited, and looked around:
Nothing was seen, but utterances could be heard:

Those of the goddess whose shrine was beneath the pile
Of the God with the baldachined altar overhead:
"And what did you get by raising this nave and aisle
Close on the site of the temple I tenanted?

"The notes of your organ have thrilled down out of view
To the earth-clogged wrecks of my edifice many a year,
Though stately and shining once--ay, long ere you
Had set up crucifix and candle here.

"Your priests have trampled the dust of mine without rueing,
Despising the joys of man whom I so much loved,
Though my springs boil on by your Gothic arcades and pewing,
And sculptures crude . . . Would Jove they could be removed!"

"--Repress, O lady proud, your traditional ires;
You know not by what a frail thread we equally hang;
It is said we are images both--twitched by people's desires;
And that I, like you, fail as a song men yesterday sang!"

* * *

And the olden dark hid the cavities late laid bare,
And all was suspended and soundless as before,
Except for a gossamery noise fading off in the air,
And the boiling voice of the waters' medicinal pour.

BATH.

SEVENTY-FOUR AND TWENTY

Here goes a man of seventy-four,
Who sees not what life means for him,
And here another in years a score
Who reads its very figure and trim.

The one who shall walk to-day with me
Is not the youth who gazes far,
But the breezy wight who cannot see
What Earth's ingrained conditions are.

THE ELOPEMENT

"A woman never agreed to it!" said my knowing friend to me.
"That one thing she'd refuse to do for Solomon's mines in fee:
No woman ever will make herself look older than she is."
I did not answer; but I thought, "you err there, ancient Quiz."

It took a rare one, true, to do it; for she was surely rare -
As rare a soul at that sweet time of her life as she was fair.
And urging motives, too, were strong, for ours was a passionate
case,
Yea, passionate enough to lead to freaking with that young face.

I have told no one about it, should perhaps make few believe,
But I think it over now that life looms dull and years bereave,
How blank we stood at our bright wits' end, two frail barks in
distress,
How self-regard in her was slain by her large tenderness.

I said: "The only chance for us in a crisis of this kind
Is going it thorough!"--"Yes," she calmly breathed. "Well, I don't
mind."
And we blanched her dark locks ruthlessly: set wrinkles on her
brow;
Ay--she was a right rare woman then, whatever she may be now.

That night we heard a coach drive up, and questions asked below.
"A gent with an elderly wife, sir," was returned from the bureau.
And the wheels went rattling on, and free at last from public ken
We washed all off in her chamber and restored her youth again.

How many years ago it was! Some fifty can it be
Since that adventure held us, and she played old wife to me?
But in time convention won her, as it wins all women at last,
And now she is rich and respectable, and time has buried the past.

"I ROSE UP AS MY CUSTOM IS"

I rose up as my custom is
   On the eve of All-Souls' day,
And left my grave for an hour or so
To call on those I used to know
   Before I passed away.

I visited my former Love
   As she lay by her husband's side;
I asked her if life pleased her, now
She was rid of a poet wrung in brow,
   And crazed with the ills he eyed;

Who used to drag her here and there
   Wherever his fancies led,
And point out pale phantasmal things,
And talk of vain vague purposings
   That she discredited.

She was quite civil, and replied,
  "Old comrade, is that you?
Well, on the whole, I like my life. -
I know I swore I'd be no wife,
  But what was I to do?

"You see, of all men for my sex
  A poet is the worst;
Women are practical, and they
Crave the wherewith to pay their way,
  And slake their social thirst.

"You were a poet--quite the ideal
  That we all love awhile:
But look at this man snoring here -
He's no romantic chanticleer,
  Yet keeps me in good style.

"He makes no quest into my thoughts,
  But a poet wants to know
What one has felt from earliest days,
Why one thought not in other ways,
  And one's Loves of long ago."

Her words benumbed my fond frail ghost;
  The nightmares neighed from their stalls
The vampires screeched, the harpies flew,
And under the dim dawn I withdrew
  To Death's inviolate halls.

A WEEK

On Monday night I closed my door,
And thought you were not as heretofore,
And little cared if we met no more.

I seemed on Tuesday night to trace
Something beyond mere commonplace
In your ideas, and heart, and face.

On Wednesday I did not opine
Your life would ever be one with mine,
Though if it were we should well combine.

On Thursday noon I liked you well,
And fondly felt that we must dwell
Not far apart, whatever befell.

On Friday it was with a thrill
In gazing towards your distant vill
I owned you were my dear one still.

I saw you wholly to my mind
On Saturday--even one who shrined
All that was best of womankind.

As wing-clipt sea-gull for the sea
On Sunday night I longed for thee,
Without whom life were waste to me!

HAD YOU WEPT

Had you wept; had you but neared me with a frail uncertain ray,
Dewy as the face of the dawn, in your large and luminous eye,
Then would have come back all the joys the tidings had slain that
day,
And a new beginning, a fresh fair heaven, have smoothed the things
awry.
But you were less feebly human, and no passionate need for clinging
Possessed your soul to overthrow reserve when I came near;
Ay, though you suffer as much as I from storms the hours are
bringing
Upon your heart and mine, I never see you shed a tear.

The deep strong woman is weakest, the weak one is the strong;
The weapon of all weapons best for winning, you have not used;
Have you never been able, or would you not, through the evil times
and long?
Has not the gift been given you, or such gift have you refused?
When I bade me not absolve you on that evening or the morrow,
Why did you not make war on me with those who weep like rain?
You felt too much, so gained no balm for all your torrid sorrow,
And hence our deep division, and our dark undying pain.

BEREFT, SHE THINKS SHE DREAMS

I dream that the dearest I ever knew
  Has died and been entombed.
I am sure it's a dream that cannot be true,
  But I am so overgloomed
By its persistence, that I would gladly
  Have quick death take me,
Rather than longer think thus sadly;
  So wake me, wake me!

It has lasted days, but minute and hour
  I expect to get aroused
And find him as usual in the bower
  Where we so happily housed.
Yet stays this nightmare too appalling,
  And like a web shakes me,
And piteously I keep on calling,
  And no one wakes me!

IN THE BRITISH MUSEUM

"What do you see in that time-touched stone,
    When nothing is there
But ashen blankness, although you give it
    A rigid stare?

"You look not quite as if you saw,
    But as if you heard,
Parting your lips, and treading softly
    As mouse or bird.

"It is only the base of a pillar, they'll tell you,
    That came to us
From a far old hill men used to name
    Areopagus."

- "I know no art, and I only view
    A stone from a wall,
But I am thinking that stone has echoed
    The voice of Paul,

"Paul as he stood and preached beside it
    Facing the crowd,
A small gaunt figure with wasted features,
    Calling out loud

"Words that in all their intimate accents
    Pattered upon
That marble front, and were far reflected,
    And then were gone.

"I'm a labouring man, and know but little,
  Or nothing at all;
But I can't help thinking that stone once echoed
  The voice of Paul."

IN THE SERVANTS' QUARTERS

"Man, you too, aren't you, one of these rough followers of the
criminal?
All hanging hereabout to gather how he's going to bear
Examination in the hall." She flung disdainful glances on
The shabby figure standing at the fire with others there,
  Who warmed them by its flare.

"No indeed, my skipping maiden: I know nothing of the trial here,
Or criminal, if so he be.--I chanced to come this way,
And the fire shone out into the dawn, and morning airs are cold now;
I, too, was drawn in part by charms I see before me play,
  That I see not every day."

"Ha, ha!" then laughed the constables who also stood to warm
themselves,
The while another maiden scrutinized his features hard,
As the blaze threw into contrast every line and knot that wrinkled
them,
Exclaiming, "Why, last night when he was brought in by the guard,
  You were with him in the yard!"

"Nay, nay, you teasing wench, I say! You know you speak mistakenly.
Cannot a tired pedestrian who has footed it afar

Here on his way from northern parts, engrossed in humble marketings,
Come in and rest awhile, although judicial doings are
   Afoot by morning star?"

"O, come, come!" laughed the constables. "Why, man, you speak the dialect
He uses in his answers; you can hear him up the stairs.
So own it. We sha'n't hurt ye. There he's speaking now! His syllables
Are those you sound yourself when you are talking unawares,
   As this pretty girl declares."

"And you shudder when his chain clinks!" she rejoined. "O yes, I noticed it.
And you winced, too, when those cuffs they gave him echoed to us here.
They'll soon be coming down, and you may then have to defend yourself
Unless you hold your tongue, or go away and keep you clear
   When he's led to judgment near!"

"No! I'll be damned in hell if I know anything about the man!
No single thing about him more than everybody knows!
Must not I even warm my hands but I am charged with blasphemies?" .
. .

- His face convulses as the morning cock that moment crows,
   And he stops, and turns, and goes.

THE OBLITERATE TOMB

"More than half my life long
Did they weigh me falsely, to my bitter wrong,
But they all have shrunk away into the silence
  Like a lost song.

"And the day has dawned and come
For forgiveness, when the past may hold it dumb
On the once reverberate words of hatred uttered
  Half in delirium . . .

"With folded lips and hands
They lie and wait what next the Will commands,
And doubtless think, if think they can: 'Let discord
  Sink with Life's sands!'

"By these late years their names,
Their virtues, their hereditary claims,
May be as near defacement at their grave-place
  As are their fames."

  --Such thoughts bechanced to seize
A traveller's mind--a man of memories -
As he set foot within the western city
  Where had died these

  Who in their lifetime deemed
Him their chief enemy--one whose brain had schemed
To get their dingy greatness deeplier dingied
  And disesteemed.

So, sojourning in their town,
He mused on them and on their once renown,
And said, "I'll seek their resting-place to-morrow
  Ere I lie down,

"And end, lest I forget,
Those ires of many years that I regret,
Renew their names, that men may see some liegeness
  Is left them yet."

Duly next day he went
And sought the church he had known them to frequent,
And wandered in the precincts, set on eyeing
  Where they lay pent,

Till by remembrance led
He stood at length beside their slighted bed,
Above which, truly, scarce a line or letter
  Could now be read.

"Thus years obliterate
Their graven worth, their chronicle, their date!
At once I'll garnish and revive the record
  Of their past state,

"That still the sage may say
In pensive progress here where they decay,
'This stone records a luminous line whose talents
  Told in their day.'"

While speaking thus he turned,
For a form shadowed where they lay inurned,
And he beheld a stranger in foreign vesture,

And tropic-burned.

"Sir, I am right pleased to view
That ancestors of mine should interest you,
For I have come of purpose here to trace them . . .
   They are time-worn, true,

"But that's a fault, at most,
Sculptors can cure. On the Pacific coast
I have vowed for long that relics of my forbears
   I'd trace ere lost,

"And hitherward I come,
Before this same old Time shall strike me numb,
To carry it out."--"Strange, this is!" said the other;
   "What mind shall plumb

"Coincident design!
Though these my father's enemies were and mine,
I nourished a like purpose--to restore them
   Each letter and line."

"Such magnanimity
Is now not needed, sir; for you will see
That since I am here, a thing like this is, plainly,
   Best done by me."

The other bowed, and left,
Crestfallen in sentiment, as one bereft
Of some fair object he had been moved to cherish,
   By hands more deft.

And as he slept that night
The phantoms of the ensepulchred stood up-right
Before him, trembling that he had set him seeking
   Their charnel-site.

And, as unknowing his ruth,
Asked as with terrors founded not on truth
Why he should want them. "Ha," they hollowly hackered,
   "You come, forsooth,

"By stealth to obliterate
Our graven worth, our chronicle, our date,
That our descendant may not gild the record
   Of our past state,

"And that no sage may say
In pensive progress near where we decay:
'This stone records a luminous line whose talents
   Told in their day.'"

Upon the morrow he went
And to that town and churchyard never bent
His ageing footsteps till, some twelvemonths onward,
   An accident

Once more detained him there;
And, stirred by hauntings, he must needs repair
To where the tomb was. Lo, it stood still wasting
   In no man's care.

"The travelled man you met
The last time," said the sexton, "has not yet
Appeared again, though wealth he had in plenty.

--Can he forget?

"The architect was hired
And came here on smart summons as desired,
But never the descendant came to tell him
  What he required."

  And so the tomb remained
Untouched, untended, crumbling, weather-stained,
And though the one-time foe was fain to right it
  He still refrained.

  "I'll set about it when
I am sure he'll come no more. Best wait till then."
But so it was that never the stranger entered
  That city again.

  And the well-meaner died
While waiting tremulously unsatisfied
That no return of the family's foreign scion
  Would still betide.

  And many years slid by,
And active church-restorers cast their eye
Upon the ancient garth and hoary building
  The tomb stood nigh.

  And when they had scraped each wall,
Pulled out the stately pews, and smartened all,
"It will be well," declared the spruce church-warden,
  "To overhaul

"And broaden this path where shown;
Nothing prevents it but an old tombstone
Pertaining to a family forgotten,
  Of deeds unknown.

"Their names can scarce be read,
Depend on't, all who care for them are dead."
So went the tomb, whose shards were as path-paving
  Distributed.

  Over it and about
Men's footsteps beat, and wind and water-spout,
Until the names, aforetime gnawed by weathers,
  Were quite worn out.

  So that no sage can say
In pensive progress near where they decay,
"This stone records a luminous line whose talents
  Told in their day."

"REGRET NOT ME"

  Regret not me;
  Beneath the sunny tree
I lie uncaring, slumbering peacefully.

  Swift as the light
  I flew my faery flight;
Ecstatically I moved, and feared no night.

I did not know
That heydays fade and go,
But deemed that what was would be always so.

I skipped at morn
Between the yellowing corn,
Thinking it good and glorious to be born.

I ran at eves
Among the piled-up sheaves,
Dreaming, "I grieve not, therefore nothing grieves."

Now soon will come
The apple, pear, and plum
And hinds will sing, and autumn insects hum.

Again you will fare
To cider-makings rare,
And junketings; but I shall not be there.

Yet gaily sing
Until the pewter ring
Those songs we sang when we went gipsying.

And lightly dance
Some triple-timed romance
In coupled figures, and forget mischance;

And mourn not me
Beneath the yellowing tree;
For I shall mind not, slumbering peacefully.

THE RECALCITRANTS

Let us off and search, and find a place
Where yours and mine can be natural lives,
Where no one comes who dissects and dives
And proclaims that ours is a curious case,
That its touch of romance can scarcely grace.

You would think it strange at first, but then
Everything has been strange in its time.
When some one said on a day of the prime
He would bow to no brazen god again
He doubtless dazed the mass of men.

None will recognize us as a pair whose claims
To righteous judgment we care not making;
Who have doubted if breath be worth the taking,
And have no respect for the current fames
Whence the savour has flown while abide the names.

We have found us already shunned, disdained,
And for re-acceptance have not once striven;
Whatever offence our course has given
The brunt thereof we have long sustained.
Well, let us away, scorned unexplained.

STARLINGS ON THE ROOF

"No smoke spreads out of this chimney-pot,
The people who lived here have left the spot,
And others are coming who knew them not.

If you listen anon, with an ear intent,
The voices, you'll find, will be different
From the well-known ones of those who went."

"Why did they go? Their tones so bland
Were quite familiar to our band;
The comers we shall not understand."

"They look for a new life, rich and strange;
They do not know that, let them range
Wherever they may, they will get no change.

"They will drag their house-gear ever so far
In their search for a home no miseries mar;
They will find that as they were they are,

"That every hearth has a ghost, alack,
And can be but the scene of a bivouac
Till they move perforce--no time to pack!"

THE MOON LOOKS IN

I

I have risen again,
And awhile survey
By my chilly ray
Through your window-pane
Your upturned face,
As you think, "Ah-she
Now dreams of me
In her distant place!"

II

I pierce her blind
In her far-off home:
She fixes a comb,
And says in her mind,
"I start in an hour;
Whom shall I meet?
Won't the men be sweet,
And the women sour!"

THE SWEET HUSSY

In his early days he was quite surprised
When she told him she was compromised
By meetings and lingerings at his whim,
And thinking not of herself but him;
While she lifted orbs aggrieved and round
That scandal should so soon abound,
(As she had raised them to nine or ten
Of antecedent nice young men)
And in remorse he thought with a sigh,
How good she is, and how bad am I! -
It was years before he understood
That she was the wicked one--he the good.

THE TELEGRAM

"O he's suffering--maybe dying--and I not there to aid,
And smooth his bed and whisper to him! Can I nohow go?
Only the nurse's brief twelve words thus hurriedly conveyed,
    As by stealth, to let me know.

"He was the best and brightest!--candour shone upon his brow,
And I shall never meet again a soldier such as he,
And I loved him ere I knew it, and perhaps he's sinking now,
    Far, far removed from me!"

- The yachts ride mute at anchor and the fulling moon is fair,
And the giddy folk are strutting up and down the smooth parade,
And in her wild distraction she seems not to be aware
   That she lives no more a maid,

But has vowed and wived herself to one who blessed the ground she trod
To and from his scene of ministry, and thought her history known
In its last particular to him--aye, almost as to God,
   And believed her quite his own.

So great her absentmindedness she droops as in a swoon,
And a movement of aversion mars her recent spousal grace,
And in silence we two sit here in our waning honeymoon
   At this idle watering-place . . .

What now I see before me is a long lane overhung
With lovelessness, and stretching from the present to the grave.
And I would I were away from this, with friends I knew when young,
   Ere a woman held me slave.

THE MOTH-SIGNAL
(On Egdon Heath)

"What are you still, still thinking,"
  He asked in vague surmise,
"That stare at the wick unblinking
  With those great lost luminous eyes?"

"O, I see a poor moth burning
  In the candle-flame," said she,
Its wings and legs are turning
  To a cinder rapidly."

"Moths fly in from the heather,"
  He said, "now the days decline."
"I know," said she. "The weather,
  I hope, will at last be fine.

"I think," she added lightly,
  "I'll look out at the door.
The ring the moon wears nightly
  May be visible now no more."

She rose, and, little heeding,
  Her husband then went on
With his attentive reading
  In the annals of ages gone.

Outside the house a figure
  Came from the tumulus near,
And speedily waxed bigger,

And clasped and called her Dear.

"I saw the pale-winged token
  You sent through the crack," sighed she.
"That moth is burnt and broken
  With which you lured out me.

"And were I as the moth is
  It might be better far
For one whose marriage troth is
  Shattered as potsherds are!"

Then grinned the Ancient Briton
  From the tumulus treed with pine:
"So, hearts are thwartly smitten
  In these days as in mine!"

SEEN BY THE WAITS

Through snowy woods and shady
  We went to play a tune
To the lonely manor-lady
  By the light of the Christmas moon.

We violed till, upward glancing
  To where a mirror leaned,
We saw her airily dancing,
  Deeming her movements screened;

Dancing alone in the room there,
  Thin-draped in her robe of night;
Her postures, glassed in the gloom there,
  Were a strange phantasmal sight.

She had learnt (we heard when homing)
  That her roving spouse was dead;
Why she had danced in the gloaming
  We thought, but never said.

THE TWO SOLDIERS

Just at the corner of the wall
  We met--yes, he and I -
Who had not faced in camp or hall
  Since we bade home good-bye,
And what once happened came back--all -
  Out of those years gone by.

And that strange woman whom we knew
  And loved--long dead and gone,
Whose poor half-perished residue,
  Tombless and trod, lay yon!
But at this moment to our view
  Rose like a phantom wan.

And in his fixed face I could see,
  Lit by a lurid shine,
The drama re-enact which she
  Had dyed incarnadine

For us, and more. And doubtless he
  Beheld it too in mine.

A start, as at one slightly known,
  And with an indifferent air
We passed, without a sign being shown
  That, as it real were,
A memory-acted scene had thrown
  Its tragic shadow there.

THE DEATH OF REGRET

I opened my shutter at sunrise,
  And looked at the hill hard by,
And I heartily grieved for the comrade
  Who wandered up there to die.

I let in the morn on the morrow,
  And failed not to think of him then,
As he trod up that rise in the twilight,
  And never came down again.

I undid the shutter a week thence,
  But not until after I'd turned
Did I call back his last departure
  By the upland there discerned.

Uncovering the casement long later,
  I bent to my toil till the gray,
When I said to myself, "Ah--what ails me,

To forget him all the day!"

As daily I flung back the shutter
  In the same blank bald routine,
He scarcely once rose to remembrance
  Through a month of my facing the scene.

And ah, seldom now do I ponder
  At the window as heretofore
On the long valued one who died yonder,
  And wastes by the sycamore.

IN THE DAYS OF CRINOLINE

A plain tilt-bonnet on her head
She took the path across the leaze.
- Her spouse the vicar, gardening, said,
"Too dowdy that, for coquetries,
  So I can hoe at ease.

But when she had passed into the heath,
And gained the wood beyond the flat,
She raised her skirts, and from beneath
Unpinned and drew as from a sheath
  An ostrich-feathered hat.

And where the hat had hung she now
Concealed and pinned the dowdy hood,
And set the hat upon her brow,
And thus emerging from the wood

Tripped on in jaunty mood.

The sun was low and crimson-faced
As two came that way from the town,
And plunged into the wood untraced . . .
When separately therefrom they paced
 The sun had quite gone down.

The hat and feather disappeared,
The dowdy hood again was donned,
And in the gloom the fair one neared
Her home and husband dour, who conned
 Calmly his blue-eyed blonde.

"To-day," he said, "you have shown good sense,
A dress so modest and so meek
Should always deck your goings hence
Alone." And as a recompense
 He kissed her on the cheek.

THE ROMAN GRAVEMOUNDS

By Rome's dim relics there walks a man,
Eyes bent; and he carries a basket and spade;
I guess what impels him to scrape and scan;
Yea, his dreams of that Empire long decayed.

"Vast was Rome," he must muse, "in the world's regard,
Vast it looms there still, vast it ever will be;"
And he stoops as to dig and unmine some shard

Left by those who are held in such memory.

But no; in his basket, see, he has brought
A little white furred thing, stiff of limb,
Whose life never won from the world a thought;
It is this, and not Rome, that is moving him.

And to make it a grave he has come to the spot,
And he delves in the ancient dead's long home;
Their fames, their achievements, the man knows not;
The furred thing is all to him--nothing Rome!

"Here say you that Caesar's warriors lie? -
But my little white cat was my only friend!
Could she but live, might the record die
Of Caesar, his legions, his aims, his end!"

Well, Rome's long rule here is oft and again
A theme for the sages of history,
And the small furred life was worth no one's pen;
Yet its mourner's mood has a charm for me.

November 1910.

THE WORKBOX

"See, here's the workbox, little wife,
    That I made of polished oak."
He was a joiner, of village life;
    She came of borough folk.

He holds the present up to her
As with a smile she nears
And answers to the profferer,
"'Twill last all my sewing years!"

"I warrant it will. And longer too.
'Tis a scantling that I got
Off poor John Wayward's coffin, who
Died of they knew not what.

"The shingled pattern that seems to cease
Against your box's rim
Continues right on in the piece
That's underground with him.

"And while I worked it made me think
Of timber's varied doom;
One inch where people eat and drink,
The next inch in a tomb.

"But why do you look so white, my dear,
And turn aside your face?
You knew not that good lad, I fear,
Though he came from your native place?"

"How could I know that good young man,
Though he came from my native town,
When he must have left there earlier than
I was a woman grown?"

"Ah no. I should have understood!
It shocked you that I gave
To you one end of a piece of wood
Whose other is in a grave?"

"Don't, dear, despise my intellect,
Mere accidental things
Of that sort never have effect
On my imaginings."

Yet still her lips were limp and wan,
Her face still held aside,
As if she had known not only John,
But known of what he died.

THE SACRILEGE
A BALLAD-TRAGEDY
(Circa 182-)

PART I

"I have a Love I love too well
Where Dunkery frowns on Exon Moor;
I have a Love I love too well,
　To whom, ere she was mine,
'Such is my love for you,' I said,
'That you shall have to hood your head
A silken kerchief crimson-red,
　Wove finest of the fine.'

"And since this Love, for one mad moon,
On Exon Wild by Dunkery Tor,
Since this my Love for one mad moon
　Did clasp me as her king,
I snatched a silk-piece red and rare
From off a stall at Priddy Fair,
For handkerchief to hood her hair
　When we went gallanting.

"Full soon the four weeks neared their end
Where Dunkery frowns on Exon Moor;
And when the four weeks neared their end,
　And their swift sweets outwore,
I said, 'What shall I do to own
Those beauties bright as tulips blown,

And keep you here with me alone
  As mine for evermore?'

"And as she drowsed within my van
On Exon Wild by Dunkery Tor -
And as she drowsed within my van,
  And dawning turned to day,
She heavily raised her sloe-black eyes
And murmured back in softest wise,
'One more thing, and the charms you prize
  Are yours henceforth for aye.

"'And swear I will I'll never go
While Dunkery frowns on Exon Moor
To meet the Cornish Wrestler Joe
  For dance and dallyings.
If you'll to yon cathedral shrine,
And finger from the chest divine
Treasure to buy me ear-drops fine,
  And richly jewelled rings.'

"I said: 'I am one who has gathered gear
From Marlbury Downs to Dunkery Tor,
Who has gathered gear for many a year
  From mansion, mart and fair;
But at God's house I've stayed my hand,
Hearing within me some command -
Curbed by a law not of the land
  From doing damage there.'

"Whereat she pouts, this Love of mine,
As Dunkery frowns on Exon Moor,
And still she pouts, this Love of mine,

So cityward I go.
But ere I start to do the thing,
And speed my soul's imperilling
For one who is my ravishing
   And all the joy I know,

"I come to lay this charge on thee -
On Exon Wild by Dunkery Tor -
I come to lay this charge on thee
   With solemn speech and sign:
Should things go ill, and my life pay
For botchery in this rash assay,
You are to take hers likewise--yea,
   The month the law takes mine.

"For should my rival, Wrestler Joe,
Where Dunkery frowns on Exon Moor -
My reckless rival, Wrestler Joe,
   My Love's possessor be,
My tortured spirit would not rest,
But wander weary and distrest
Throughout the world in wild protest:
   The thought nigh maddens me!"

PART II

Thus did he speak--this brother of mine -
On Exon Wild by Dunkery Tor,
Born at my birth of mother of mine,
   And forthwith went his way
To dare the deed some coming night . . .
I kept the watch with shaking sight,

The moon at moments breaking bright,
　At others glooming gray.

For three full days I heard no sound
Where Dunkery frowns on Exon Moor,
I heard no sound at all around
　Whether his fay prevailed,
Or one malign the master were,
Till some afoot did tidings bear
How that, for all his practised care,
　He had been caught and jailed.

They had heard a crash when twelve had chimed
By Mendip east of Dunkery Tor,
When twelve had chimed and moonlight climbed;
　They watched, and he was tracked
By arch and aisle and saint and knight
Of sculptured stonework sheeted white
In the cathedral's ghostly light,
　And captured in the act.

Yes; for this Love he loved too well
Where Dunkery sights the Severn shore,
All for this Love he loved too well
　He burst the holy bars,
Seized golden vessels from the chest
To buy her ornaments of the best,
At her ill-witchery's request
　And lure of eyes like stars . . .

When blustering March confused the sky
In Toneborough Town by Exon Moor,
When blustering March confused the sky

They stretched him; and he died.
Down in the crowd where I, to see
The end of him, stood silently,
    With a set face he lipped to me -
"Remember." "Ay!" I cried.

By night and day I shadowed her
From Toneborough Deane to Dunkery Tor,
I shadowed her asleep, astir,
    And yet I could not bear -
Till Wrestler Joe anon began
To figure as her chosen man,
And took her to his shining van -
    To doom a form so fair!

He made it handsome for her sake -
And Dunkery smiled to Exon Moor -
He made it handsome for her sake,
    Painting it out and in;
And on the door of apple-green
A bright brass knocker soon was seen,
And window-curtains white and clean
    For her to sit within.

And all could see she clave to him
As cleaves a cloud to Dunkery Tor,
Yea, all could see she clave to him,
    And every day I said,
"A pity it seems to part those two
That hourly grow to love more true:
Yet she's the wanton woman who
    Sent one to swing till dead!"

That blew to blazing all my hate,
While Dunkery frowned on Exon Moor,
And when the river swelled, her fate
  Came to her pitilessly . . .
I dogged her, crying: "Across that plank
They use as bridge to reach yon bank
A coat and hat lie limp and dank;
  Your goodman's, can they be?"

She paled, and went, I close behind -
And Exon frowned to Dunkery Tor,
She went, and I came up behind
  And tipped the plank that bore
Her, fleetly flitting across to eye
What such might bode. She slid awry;
And from the current came a cry,
  A gurgle; and no more.

How that befell no mortal knew
From Marlbury Downs to Exon Moor;
No mortal knew that deed undue
  But he who schemed the crime,
Which night still covers . . . But in dream
Those ropes of hair upon the stream
He sees, and he will hear that scream
  Until his judgment-time.

THE ABBEY MASON

(Inventor of the "Perpendicular" Style of Gothic Architecture)

The new-vamped Abbey shaped apace
In the fourteenth century of grace;

(The church which, at an after date,
Acquired cathedral rank and state.)

Panel and circumscribing wall
Of latest feature, trim and tall,

Rose roundabout the Norman core
In prouder pose than theretofore,

Encasing magically the old
With parpend ashlars manifold.

The trowels rang out, and tracery
Appeared where blanks had used to be.

Men toiled for pleasure more than pay,
And all went smoothly day by day,

Till, in due course, the transept part
Engrossed the master-mason's art.

- Home-coming thence he tossed and turned
Throughout the night till the new sun burned.

"What fearful visions have inspired
These gaingivings?" his wife inquired;

"As if your tools were in your hand
You have hammered, fitted, muttered, planned;

"You have thumped as you were working hard:
I might have found me bruised and scarred.

"What then's amiss. What eating care
Looms nigh, whereof I am unaware?"

He answered not, but churchward went,
Viewing his draughts with discontent;

And fumbled there the livelong day
Till, hollow-eyed, he came away.

- 'Twas said, "The master-mason's ill!"
And all the abbey works stood still.

Quoth Abbot Wygmore: "Why, O why
Distress yourself? You'll surely die!"

The mason answered, trouble-torn,
"This long-vogued style is quite outworn!

"The upper archmould nohow serves
To meet the lower tracery curves:

"The ogees bend too far away
To give the flexures interplay.

"This it is causes my distress . . .
So it will ever be unless

"New forms be found to supersede
The circle when occasions need.

"To carry it out I have tried and toiled,
And now perforce must own me foiled!

"Jeerers will say: 'Here was a man
Who could not end what he began!'"

- So passed that day, the next, the next;
The abbot scanned the task, perplexed;

The townsmen mustered all their wit
To fathom how to compass it,

But no raw artistries availed
Where practice in the craft had failed . . .

- One night he tossed, all open-eyed,
And early left his helpmeet's side.

Scattering the rushes of the floor
He wandered from the chamber door

And sought the sizing pile, whereon
Struck dimly a cadaverous dawn

Through freezing rain, that drenched the board
Of diagram-lines he last had scored -

Chalked phantasies in vain begot
To knife the architectural knot -

In front of which he dully stood,
Regarding them in hopeless mood.

He closelier looked; then looked again:
The chalk-scratched draught-board faced the rain,

Whose icicled drops deformed the lines
Innumerous of his lame designs,

So that they streamed in small white threads
From the upper segments to the heads

Of arcs below, uniting them
Each by a stalactitic stem.

- At once, with eyes that struck out sparks,
He adds accessory cusping-marks,

Then laughs aloud. The thing was done
So long assayed from sun to sun . . .

- Now in his joy he grew aware
Of one behind him standing there,

And, turning, saw the abbot, who
The weather's whim was watching too.

Onward to Prime the abbot went,
Tacit upon the incident.

\- Men now discerned as days revolved
The ogive riddle had been solved;

Templates were cut, fresh lines were chalked
Where lines had been defaced and balked,

And the work swelled and mounted higher,
Achievement distancing desire;

Here jambs with transoms fixed between,
Where never the like before had been -

There little mullions thinly sawn
Where meeting circles once were drawn.

"We knew," men said, "the thing would go
After his craft-wit got aglow,

"And, once fulfilled what he has designed,
We'll honour him and his great mind!"

When matters stood thus poised awhile,
And all surroundings shed a smile,

The master-mason on an eve
Homed to his wife and seemed to grieve . . .

\- "The abbot spoke to me to-day:
He hangs about the works alway.

"He knows the source as well as I
Of the new style men magnify.

"He said: 'You pride yourself too much
On your creation. Is it such?

"'Surely the hand of God it is
That conjured so, and only His! -

"'Disclosing by the frost and rain
Forms your invention chased in vain;

"'Hence the devices deemed so great
You copied, and did not create.'

"I feel the abbot's words are just,
And that all thanks renounce I must.

"Can a man welcome praise and pelf
For hatching art that hatched itself? . . .

"So, I shall own the deft design
Is Heaven's outshaping, and not mine."

"What!" said she. "Praise your works ensure
To throw away, and quite obscure

"Your beaming and beneficent star?
Better you leave things as they are!

"Why, think awhile. Had not your zest
In your loved craft curtailed your rest -

"Had you not gone there ere the day
The sun had melted all away!"

- But, though his good wife argued so,
The mason let the people know

That not unaided sprang the thought
Whereby the glorious fane was wrought,

But that by frost when dawn was dim
The method was disclosed to him.

"Yet," said the townspeople thereat,
"'Tis your own doing, even with that!"

But he--chafed, childlike, in extremes -
The temperament of men of dreams -

Aloofly scrupled to admit
That he did aught but borrow it,

And diffidently made request
That with the abbot all should rest.

- As none could doubt the abbot's word,
Or question what the church averred,

The mason was at length believed
Of no more count than he conceived,

And soon began to lose the fame
That late had gathered round his name . . .

- Time passed, and like a living thing
The pile went on embodying,

And workmen died, and young ones grew,
And the old mason sank from view

And Abbots Wygmore and Staunton went
And Horton sped the embellishment.

But not till years had far progressed
Chanced it that, one day, much impressed,

Standing within the well-graced aisle,
He asked who first conceived the style;

And some decrepit sage detailed
How, when invention nought availed,

The cloud-cast waters in their whim
Came down, and gave the hint to him

Who struck each arc, and made each mould;
And how the abbot would not hold

As sole begetter him who applied
Forms the Almighty sent as guide;

And how the master lost renown,
And wore in death no artist's crown.

- Then Horton, who in inner thought
Had more perceptions than he taught,

Replied: "Nay; art can but transmute;
Invention is not absolute;

"Things fail to spring from nought at call,
And art-beginnings most of all.

"He did but what all artists do,
Wait upon Nature for his cue."

- "Had you been here to tell them so
Lord Abbot, sixty years ago,

"The mason, now long underground,
Doubtless a different fate had found.

"He passed into oblivion dim,
And none knew what became of him!

"His name? 'Twas of some common kind
And now has faded out of mind."

The Abbot: "It shall not be hid!
I'll trace it." . . . But he never did.

- When longer yet dank death had wormed
The brain wherein the style had germed

From Gloucester church it flew afar -
The style called Perpendicular. -

To Winton and to Westminster
It ranged, and grew still beautifuller:

From Solway Frith to Dover Strand
Its fascinations starred the land,

Not only on cathedral walls
But upon courts and castle halls,

Till every edifice in the isle
Was patterned to no other style,

And till, long having played its part,
The curtain fell on Gothic art.

- Well: when in Wessex on your rounds,
Take a brief step beyond its bounds,

And enter Gloucester: seek the quoin
Where choir and transept interjoin,

And, gazing at the forms there flung
Against the sky by one unsung -

The ogee arches transom-topped,
The tracery-stalks by spandrels stopped,

Petrified lacework--lightly lined
On ancient massiveness behind -

Muse that some minds so modest be
As to renounce fame's fairest fee,

(Like him who crystallized on this spot
His visionings, but lies forgot,

And many a mediaeval one
Whose symmetries salute the sun)

While others boom a baseless claim,
And upon nothing rear a name.

THE JUBILEE OF A MAGAZINE
(To the Editor)

Yes; your up-dated modern page -
All flower-fresh, as it appears -
Can claim a time-tried lineage,

That reaches backward fifty years
(Which, if but short for sleepy squires,
Is much in magazines' careers).

- Here, on your cover, never tires
The sower, reaper, thresher, while
As through the seasons of our sires

Each wills to work in ancient style
With seedlip, sickle, share and flail,
Though modes have since moved many a mile!

The steel-roped plough now rips the vale,
With cog and tooth the sheaves are won,
Wired wheels drum out the wheat like hail;

But if we ask, what has been done
To unify the mortal lot
Since your bright leaves first saw the sun,

Beyond mechanic furtherance--what
Advance can rightness, candour, claim?
Truth bends abashed, and answers not.

Despite your volumes' gentle aim
To straighten visions wry and wrong,
Events jar onward much the same!

- Had custom tended to prolong,
As on your golden page engrained,
Old processes of blade and prong,

And best invention been retained
For high crusades to lessen tears
Throughout the race, the world had gained! . . .
But too much, this, for fifty years.

THE SATIN SHOES

"If ever I walk to church to wed,
  As other maidens use,
And face the gathered eyes," she said,
  "I'll go in satin shoes!"

She was as fair as early day
  Shining on meads unmown,
And her sweet syllables seemed to play
  Like flute-notes softly blown.

The time arrived when it was meet

That she should be a bride;
The satin shoes were on her feet,
   Her father was at her side.

They stood within the dairy door,
   And gazed across the green;
The church loomed on the distant moor,
   But rain was thick between.

"The grass-path hardly can be stepped,
   The lane is like a pool!" -
Her dream is shown to be inept,
   Her wish they overrule.

"To go forth shod in satin soft
   A coach would be required!"
For thickest boots the shoes were doffed -
   Those shoes her soul desired . . .

All day the bride, as overborne,
   Was seen to brood apart,
And that the shoes had not been worn
   Sat heavy on her heart.

From her wrecked dream, as months flew on,
   Her thought seemed not to range.
What ails the wife?" they said anon,
   "That she should be so strange?" . . .

Ah--what coach comes with furtive glide -
   A coach of closed-up kind?
It comes to fetch the last year's bride,
   Who wanders in her mind.

She strove with them, and fearfully ran
  Stairward with one low scream:
"Nay--coax her," said the madhouse man,
  "With some old household theme."

"If you will go, dear, you must fain
  Put on those shoes--the pair
Meant for your marriage, which the rain
  Forbade you then to wear."

She clapped her hands, flushed joyous hues;
  "O yes--I'll up and ride
If I am to wear my satin shoes
  And be a proper bride!"

Out then her little foot held she,
  As to depart with speed;
The madhouse man smiled pleasantly
  To see the wile succeed.

She turned to him when all was done,
  And gave him her thin hand,
Exclaiming like an enraptured one,
  "This time it will be grand!"

She mounted with a face elate,
  Shut was the carriage door;
They drove her to the madhouse gate,
  And she was seen no more . . .

Yet she was fair as early day
  Shining on meads unmown,

And her sweet syllables seemed to play
  Like flute-notes softly blown.

EXEUNT OMNES

I

  Everybody else, then, going,
And I still left where the fair was? . . .
Much have I seen of neighbour loungers
  Making a lusty showing,
  Each now past all knowing.

II

  There is an air of blankness
In the street and the littered spaces;
Thoroughfare, steeple, bridge and highway
  Wizen themselves to lankness;
  Kennels dribble dankness.

III

  Folk all fade. And whither,
As I wait alone where the fair was?
Into the clammy and numbing night-fog
  Whence they entered hither.
  Soon do I follow thither!

June 2, 1913.

A POET

Attentive eyes, fantastic heed,
Assessing minds, he does not need,
Nor urgent writs to sup or dine,
Nor pledges in the roseate wine.

For loud acclaim he does not care
By the august or rich or fair,
Nor for smart pilgrims from afar,
Curious on where his hauntings are.

But soon or later, when you hear
That he has doffed this wrinkled gear,
Some evening, at the first star-ray,
Come to his graveside, pause and say:

"Whatever the message his to tell,
Two bright-souled women loved him well."
Stand and say that amid the dim:
It will be praise enough for him.

July 1914.

POSTSCRIPT

"MEN WHO MARCH AWAY"
(SONG OF THE SOLDIERS)

What of the faith and fire within us
  Men who march away
  Ere the barn-cocks say
  Night is growing gray,
To hazards whence no tears can win us;
What of the faith and fire within us
  Men who march away?

Is it a purblind prank, O think you,
  Friend with the musing eye,
  Who watch us stepping by
  With doubt and dolorous sigh?
Can much pondering so hoodwink you!
Is it a purblind prank, O think you,
  Friend with the musing eye?

Nay. We well see what we are doing,
  Though some may not see -
  Dalliers as they be -

England's need are we;
Her distress would leave us rueing:
Nay. We well see what we are doing,
    Though some may not see!

In our heart of hearts believing
    Victory crowns the just,
    And that braggarts must
    Surely bite the dust,
Press we to the field ungrieving,
In our heart of hearts believing
    Victory crowns the just.

Hence the faith and fire within us
    Men who march away
    Ere the barn-cocks say
    Night is growing gray,
To hazards whence no tears can win us:
Hence the faith and fire within us
    Men who march away.

September 5, 1914.

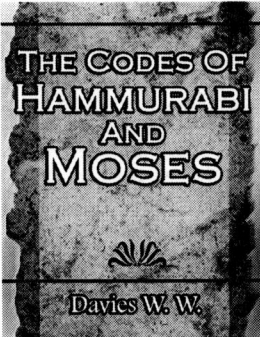

The Codes Of Hammurabi And Moses
W. W. Davies

QTY

The discovery of the Hammurabi Code is one of the greatest achievements of archaeology, and is of paramount interest, not only to the student of the Bible, but also to all those interested in ancient history...

Religion **ISBN:** *1-59462-338-4* **Pages:132**
MSRP $12.95

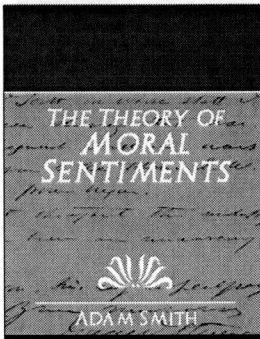

The Theory of Moral Sentiments
Adam Smith

QTY

This work from 1749. contains original theories of conscience amd moral judgment and it is the foundation for systemof morals.

Philosophy **ISBN:** *1-59462-777-0* **Pages:536**
MSRP $19.95

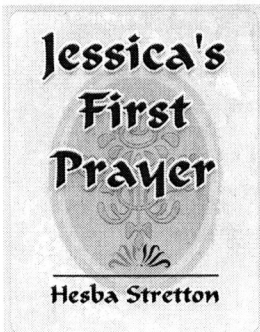

Jessica's First Prayer
Hesba Stretton

QTY

In a screened and secluded corner of one of the many railway-bridges which span the streets of London there could be seen a few years ago, from five o'clock every morning until half past eight, a tidily set-out coffee-stall, consisting of a trestle and board, upon which stood two large tin cans, with a small fire of charcoal burning under each so as to keep the coffee boiling during the early hours of the morning when the work-people were thronging into the city on their way to their daily toil...

Pages:84

Childrens **ISBN:** *1-59462-373-2* *MSRP $9.95*

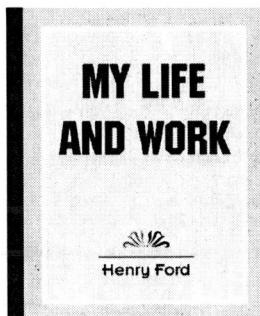

My Life and Work
Henry Ford

QTY

Henry Ford revolutionized the world with his implementation of mass production for the Model T automobile. Gain valuable business insight into his life and work with his own auto-biography... "We have only started on our development of our country we have not as yet, with all our talk of wonderful progress, done more than scratch the surface. The progress has been wonderful enough but..."

Pages:300

Biographies/ **ISBN:** *1-59462-198-5* *MSRP $21.95*

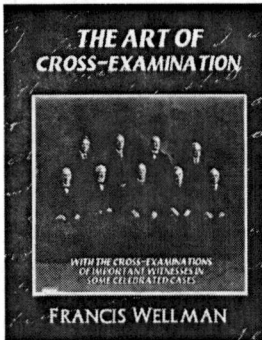

The Art of Cross-Examination
Francis Wellman

QTY

I presume it is the experience of every author, after his first book is published upon an important subject, to be almost overwhelmed with a wealth of ideas and illustrations which could readily have been included in his book, and which to his own mind, at least, seem to make a second edition inevitable. Such certainly was the case with me; and when the first edition had reached its sixth impression in five months, I rejoiced to learn that it seemed to my publishers that the book had met with a sufficiently favorable reception to justify a second and considerably enlarged edition. ...

Pages:412

Reference   ISBN: *1-59462-647-2*   *MSRP $19.95*

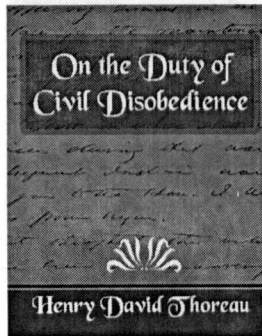

On the Duty of Civil Disobedience
Henry David Thoreau

QTY

Thoreau wrote his famous essay, On the Duty of Civil Disobedience, as a protest against an unjust but popular war and the immoral but popular institution of slave-owning. He did more than write—he declined to pay his taxes, and was hauled off to gaol in consequence. Who can say how much this refusal of his hastened the end of the war and of slavery ?

Pages:48

Law   ISBN: *1-59462-747-9*   *MSRP $7.45*

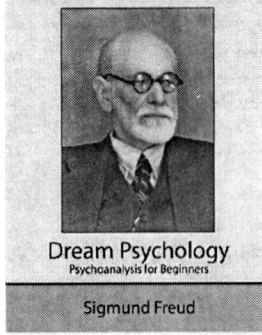

Dream Psychology Psychoanalysis for Beginners
Sigmund Freud

QTY

Sigmund Freud, born Sigismund Schlomo Freud (May 6, 1856 - September 23, 1939), was a Jewish-Austrian neurologist and psychiatrist who co-founded the psychoanalytic school of psychology. Freud is best known for his theories of the unconscious mind, especially involving the mechanism of repression; his redefinition of sexual desire as mobile and directed towards a wide variety of objects; and his therapeutic techniques, especially his understanding of transference in the therapeutic relationship and the presumed value of dreams as sources of insight into unconscious desires.

Pages:196

Psychology   ISBN: *1-59462-905-6*   *MSRP $15.45*

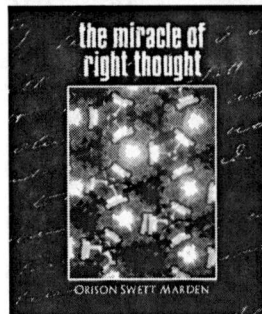

The Miracle of Right Thought
Orison Swett Marden

QTY

Believe with all of your heart that you will do what you were made to do. When the mind has once formed the habit of holding cheerful, happy, prosperous pictures, it will not be easy to form the opposite habit. ·It does not matter how improbable or how far away this realization may see, or how dark the prospects may be, if we visualize them as best we can, as vividly as possible, hold tenaciously to them and vigorously struggle to attain them, they will gradually become actualized, realized in the life. But a desire, a longing without endeavor, a yearning abandoned or held indifferently will vanish without realization.

Pages:360

Self Help   ISBN: *1-59462-644-8*   *MSRP $25.45*

QTY

☐ **The Rosicrucian Cosmo-Conception Mystic Christianity** *by Max Heindel*   ISBN: *1-59462-188-8*   **$38.95**
The Rosicrucian Cosmo-conception is not dogmatic, neither does it appeal to any other authority than the reason of the student. It is: not controversial, but is: sent forth in the, hope that it may help to clear..   New Age/Religion Pages 646

☐ **Abandonment To Divine Providence** *by Jean-Pierre de Caussade*   ISBN: *1-59462-228-0*   **$25.95**
"The Rev. Jean Pierre de Caussade was one of the most remarkable spiritual writers of the Society of Jesus in France in the 18th Century. His death took place at Toulouse in 1751. His works have gone through many editions and have been republished...   Inspirational/Religion Pages 400

☐ **Mental Chemistry** *by Charles Haanel*   ISBN: *1-59462-192-6*   **$23.95**
Mental Chemistry allows the change of material conditions by combining and appropriately utilizing the power of the mind. Much like applied chemistry creates something new and unique out of careful combinations of chemicals the mastery of mental chemistry...   New Age Pages 354

☐ **The Letters of Robert Browning and Elizabeth Barret Barrett 1845-1846 vol II**   ISBN: *1-59462-193-4*   **$35.95**
by Robert Browning and Elizabeth Barrett   Biographies Pages 596

☐ **Gleanings In Genesis (volume I)** *by Arthur W. Pink*   ISBN: *1-59462-130-6*   **$27.45**
Appropriately has Genesis been termed "the seed plot of the Bible" for in it we have, in germ form, almost all of the great doctrines which are afterwards fully developed in the books of Scripture which follow...   Religion/Inspirational Pages 420

☐ **The Master Key** *by L. W. de Laurence*   ISBN: *1-59462-001-6*   **$30.95**
In no branch of human knowledge has there been a more lively increase of the spirit of research during the past few years than in the study of Psychology, Concentration and Mental Discipline. The requests for authentic lessons in Thought Control, Mental Discipline and...   New Age/Business Pages 422

☐ **The Lesser Key Of Solomon Goetia** *by L. W. de Laurence*   ISBN: *1-59462-092-X*   **$9.95**
This translation of the first book of the "Lemegton" which is now for the first time made accessible to students of Talismanic Magic was done, after careful collation and edition, from numerous Ancient Manuscripts in Hebrew, Latin, and French...   New Age/Occult Pages 92

☐ **Rubaiyat Of Omar Khayyam** *by Edward Fitzgerald*   ISBN:*1-59462-332-5*   **$13.95**
Edward Fitzgerald, whom the world has already learned, in spite of his own efforts to remain within the shadow of anonymity, to look upon as one of the rarest poets of the century, was born at Bredfield, in Suffolk, on the 31st of March, 1809. He was the third son of John Purcell...   Music Pages 172

☐ **Ancient Law** *by Henry Maine*   ISBN: *1-59462-128-4*   **$29.95**
The chief object of the following pages is to indicate some of the earliest ideas of mankind, as they are reflected in Ancient Law, and to point out the relation of those ideas to modern thought.   Religion/History Pages 452

☐ **Far-Away Stories** *by William J. Locke*   ISBN: *1-59462-129-2*   **$19.45**
"Good wine needs no bush, but a collection of mixed vintages does. And this book is just such a collection. Some of the stories I do not want to remain buried for ever in the museum files of dead magazine-numbers an author's not unpardonable vanity..."   Fiction Pages 272

☐ **Life of David Crockett** *by David Crockett*   ISBN: *1-59462-250-7*   **$27.45**
"Colonel David Crockett was one of the most remarkable men of the times in which he lived. Born in humble life, but gifted with a strong will, an indomitable courage, and unremitting perseverance...   Biographies/New Age Pages 424

☐ **Lip-Reading** *by Edward Nitchie*   ISBN: *1-59462-206-X*   **$25.95**
Edward B. Nitchie, founder of the New York School for the Hard of Hearing, now the Nitchie School of Lip-Reading, Inc, wrote "LIP-READING Principles and Practice". The development and perfecting of this meritorious work on lip-reading was an undertaking...   How-to Pages 400

☐ **A Handbook of Suggestive Therapeutics, Applied Hypnotism, Psychic Science**   ISBN: *1-59462-214-0*   **$24.95**
by Henry Munro   Health/New Age/Health/Self-help Pages 376

☐ **A Doll's House: and Two Other Plays** *by Henrik Ibsen*   ISBN: *1-59462-112-8*   **$19.95**
Henrik Ibsen created this classic when in revolutionary 1848 Rome. Introducing some striking concepts in playwriting for the realist genre, this play has been studied the world over.   Fiction/Classics/Plays 308

☐ **The Light of Asia** *by sir Edwin Arnold*   ISBN: *1-59462-204-3*   **$13.95**
In this poetic masterpiece, Edwin Arnold describes the life and teachings of Buddha. The man who was to become known as Buddha to the world was born as Prince Gautama of India but he rejected the worldly riches and abandoned the reigns of power when... Religion/History/Biographies Pages 170

☐ **The Complete Works of Guy de Maupassant** *by Guy de Maupassant*   ISBN: *1-59462-157-8*   **$16.95**
"For days and days, nights and nights, I had dreamed of that first kiss which was to consecrate our engagement, and I knew not on what spot I should put my lips..."   Fiction/Classics Pages 240

☐ **The Art of Cross-Examination** *by Francis L. Wellman*   ISBN: *1-59462-309-6*   **$26.95**
Written by a renowned trial lawyer, Wellman imparts his experience and uses case studies to explain how to use psychology to extract desired information through questioning.   How-to/Science/Reference Pages 408

☐ **Answered or Unanswered?** *by Louisa Vaughan*   ISBN: *1-59462-248-5*   **$10.95**
Miracles of Faith in China   Religion Pages 112

☐ **The Edinburgh Lectures on Mental Science (1909)** *by Thomas*   ISBN: *1-59462-008-3*   **$11.95**
This book contains the substance of a course of lectures recently given by the writer in the Queen Street Hall, Edinburgh. Its purpose is to indicate the Natural Principles governing the relation between Mental Action and Material Conditions...   New Age/Psychology Pages 148

☐ **Ayesha** *by H. Rider Haggard*   ISBN: *1-59462-301-5*   **$24.95**
Verily and indeed it is the unexpected that happens! Probably if there was one person upon the earth from whom the Editor of this, and of a certain previous history, did not expect to hear again...   Classics Pages 380

☐ **Ayala's Angel** *by Anthony Trollope*   ISBN: *1-59462-352-X*   **$29.95**
The two girls were both pretty, but Lucy who was twenty-one who supposed to be simple and comparatively unattractive, whereas Ayala was credited, as her Bombwhat romantic name might show, with poetic charm and a taste for romance. Ayala when her father died was nineteen...   Fiction Pages 484

☐ **The American Commonwealth** *by James Bryce*   ISBN: *1-59462-286-8*   **$34.45**
An interpretation of American democratic political theory. It examines political mechanics and society from the perspective of Scotsman James Bryce   Politics Pages 572

☐ **Stories of the Pilgrims** *by Margaret P. Pumphrey*   ISBN: *1-59462-116-0*   **$17.95**
This book explores pilgrims religious oppression in England as well as their escape to Holland and eventual crossing to America on the Mayflower, and their early days in New England...   History Pages 268

CPSIA information can be obtained at www.ICGtesting.com
Printed in the USA
LVOW05s1944120814

398773LV00011B/440/P